THE IMMORTALS

THE SEASON MY MILAN TEAM REINVENTED FOOTBALL

translated from the Italian by Mark Palmer

ARRIGO SACCHI

with Luigi Garlando

BACKPAGE

First published in Great Britain in 2021
This edition published 2021 by
BACKPAGE

www.backpagepress.co.uk
@BackPagePress

Italian edition first published 2019

ISBN: 9781909430532
eBook ISBN: 9781909430549

A catalogue record for this book is available on request from the British Library.

Typeset by BackPage
Cover design by Kouki Gharra (kulbirgharra.com)
Printed in Great Britain by MBM Print

To president Berlusconi, because the dream began with him

To Adriano Galliani, who supported me

To my players, who believed

To the entire Milan 'family', who all contributed

To Giulia, Gina and Pietro – so that they know their grandfather's story

CONTENTS

MEET THE IMMORTALS

THE COACH – ARRIGO SACCHI

That Arrigo Sacchi is a founding father of modern football is not up for discussion. He was a penalty shoot-out away from bringing the World Cup from the USA to Italy in 1994, but the primary reason his place in the history of the sport is secure is the story you are about to read. When Sacchi applied the principles he had developed in his journey through the Italian lower leagues to a Milan team containing some of the best footballers of their era, the result was a team that blew the opposition away at home and in Europe, and influenced the evolution of football for generations. Milan won Serie A in Sacchi's first season as coach, and then back-to-back European Cups in the following two.

THE PRESIDENT – SILVIO BERLUSCONI

Served as prime minister of Italy in four governments between 1994 and 2011, mostly as the leader of the populist Forza Italia party. In 1988, Berlusconi was the owner of Mediaset, a conglomerate that is Italy's largest broadcaster, and the owner and president of Milan, a fallen giant he was determined to propel back to the top of Italian football.

THE CHIEF EXECUTIVE – ADRIANO GALLIANI

Berlusconi's influential right-hand man. Sacchi credits him with a huge role in helping to build the empire through shrewd strategy and dealmaking.

THE TEAM...

GIOVANNI GALLI

As Italy's starting goalkeeper at the 1986 World Cup, Galli was one of the established stars of the Milan team inherited by Sacchi and the undisputed No.1 during the run to the 1989 European Cup final. He was briefly sporting director of Hellas Verona and has worked as a pundit, but failed in a bid to follow his former employer into politics when he was defeated in the mayoral race in the city where his pro career began, Florence.

MAURO TASSOTTI

At right-back in Barcelona in May 1989, Tassotti was in the middle of an incredible 17-year career with Milan, who he had joined from Lazio as a 20-year-old. One of the core members of the side that remained beyond the Sacchi era and into that of Fabio Capello, in 1994 Tassotti captained the team to its third European title in five years and would represent the club as coach and caretaker manager after his retirement.

FRANCO BARESI

Before he was the captain of the all-conquering Milan team, Baresi was twice relegated to Serie B with the *Rossoneri*. After winning the second tier for the second time, he set about collecting more significant trophies during a 20-year, one-club career that ended with Baresi named as Milan's Player of the Century and acknowledged as one of the greatest defenders to play the game.

ALESSANDRO COSTACURTA

Barsei's apprentice played on for Milan until he was 41 and his former team-mate, Carlo Ancelotti, was now his coach. That longevity led to five European Cup and Champions League wins, and it all started in season 1988/89, when Sacchi promoted 'Billy' – the nickname came from the sponsor on the shirts of Milan's basketball team, for whom the skinny centre-back seemed a better fit – from understudy to a starring role.

PAOLO MALDINI

The final member of the quartet who made up perhaps the most formidable defence in football history was also its youngest. Maldini reached the Milan first team when he was just 16. He was *Rossoneri* royalty, the son of Cesare, a former captain, and finished a 25-year career with 902 appearances, a club record. He is now their technical director and his No.3 shirt is retired.

ANGELO COLOMBO

A rare member of the 1989 European Cup winning team who ended his career without an international cap, but highly-valued by his innovative coach. Colombo played in Serie A for Avellino and Udinese at the start of his career, and Bari at the end, but in the middle were three glorious seasons as a starter in one of the greatest sides of all time.

FRANK RIJKAARD

The man who prompted Sacchi to issue Berlusconi with an ultimatum, and with good reason. Rijkaard was the final part of the great coach's puzzle, a player as gifted as he was versatile. He won his third Champions League title in his final game as a pro – having returned to his first club, Ajax – against the club with which he won his first two: Milan.

CARLO ANCELOTTI

An entire generation now know Ancelotti only as the hangdog-faced manager of Real Madrid, Chelsea, Paris St Germain and Bayern Munich. Here we will be reacquainted with a midfielder who absorbed game intelligence with each passing season of his storied playing career. A Serie A winner with both Roma and Milan, he was the player on whose recruitment Sacchi believed the resurrection of Milan depended.

ROBERTO DONADONI

A dynamic and distinct force on the wing, Donadoni played in Milan for a decade and was as integral a part of the Italy team across two World Cup cycles. A victim of three penalty shoot-outs with the national team, Donadoni missed in the semi-final against Argentina in 1990; did not take a penalty as Italy lost the final shoot-out in '94 and lost his post as national team manager after his team took eventual winners Spain to penalties in the quarter-finals of Euro 2008.

RUUD GULLIT

If one player epitomised the Dutch ideal of an all-round footballer who could make the team function from any position in the park, perhaps it was Gullit. The dreadlocked, moustachioed lion who had captained Holland to victory at Euro 88 and won the Ballon d'Or a year earlier reached his peak in Sacchi's Milan, propelling his team through opposition defences from midfield or attack.

MARCO VAN BASTEN

The most feared No.9 of his generation played his last game at the age of 28 yet still retired with three Ballons d'Or. He had every weapon: he was 6ft 3ins, powerful and fast. Outside the box, he had the power to shoot from distance and the guile to play in a teammate; inside it, he could score acrobatic volleys and gravity-defying headers, or predatory tap-ins. A striker like no other.

THE SUBSTITUTES...

PIETRO PAOLO VIRDIS

Replaced Gullit in Barcelona to join Van Basten in a partnership that was often Sacchi's preferred pairing. Virdis was at the end of five years at Milan that saw him win the Capocannoniere award as Serie A's top goalscorer, before becoming an integral part of the new coach's revolution.

FILIPPO GALLI

Replaced Costacurta late on in the '89 final, having lost his place in the defence in which he had won Serie A a year earlier. Thereafter Galli was the fifth Beatle of that legendary backline under both Sacchi and Fabio Capello. At 38, he enjoyed a single season in English football, with Watford, and scored a single goal, against Walsall. With Tassotti, he was part of an old boys' Milan coaching staff under the returning Ancelotti in 2008.

ROBERTO MUSSI

Won the Serie C title under Sacchi at Parma before

his old coach signed him for Milan at the start of the 1987/88 season. Largely used as back-up during two glorious years with the *Rossoneri*, Mussi nonetheless proved his value after he left: he won the Coppa Italia and reached a UEFA Cup final with Torino and then won two UEFA Cups in a second spell with Parma.

ALBERICO EVANI

An academy product who had been part of the wilderness years before being led by Sacchi to the sunlit uplands of three Serie A and two European Cup triumphs. He also played in Sacchi's World Cup final, scoring in the shoot-out. During the 1988/89 season, he provided invaluable cover in the mid-season dog days, when injuries reduced Milan to the bare bones.

THE MOON ABOVE THE BELL TOWER

It may seem a little suspect for a writer who supports Inter to celebrate a European Cup won by Milan. It's like General Custer penning the biography of Sitting Bull. However, the achievements described in this book fly high above any bell tower, beyond the usual boundaries of affiliation.

Arrigo Sacchi's European Cup in 1989 was a landmark event for football, and not just in Italy. As *L'Equipe* wrote after they beat Steaua Bucharest 4-0 in the final in Barcelona, "football can no longer be the same".

That Milan team, who reworked the lessons of the great Ajax side of the 1970s with modern pressing, were trend-setters. The echo can be heard even now: without that Milan team, we would never have had Pep Guardiola's Barcelona.

For Italy, in particular, that Milan team were as innovative as Dick Fosbury, splitting history in two. Previously, you jumped stomach-first, but now you lead with the back. Previously, we won European Cups respecting a defensive tradition, and now we won them going forward, with or without the ball. Always attacking, even at the Bernabeu, seeking out the ball not to break but to keep it. All totally unheard of – a revolution.

Sacchi wasn't just concerned about the result, he told his players to shoot for the moon: he wanted beauty. For this reason, his triumph in Barcelona was something completely unprecedented, like man's first steps on the moon. Thirty-two years on, it deserves to be celebrated as such.

The three astronauts of Apollo 11, who made their moon landing in the same year as Nereo Rocco's Milan won a second European Cup*, left their mark on that satellite not as Americans, but "for all mankind".

In the same way, and keeping a sense of proportion, the 1989 success and the beauty of that Milan – judged by UEFA to be the strongest team of all time – deserve to be celebrated with a spirit of universality. Beauty gratifies all those who love the game. That team, which flourished by surprise in the orchard of our tradition, made many people fall in love, and not just Milan supporters. I was one of them.

And how much joy I found in discovering the secrets of the sorcerer, the diary that Sacchi kept day by day, noting down session plans, judgements about players and comments on matches. We reveal them all in these pages and I'm certain that footballer lovers – be they Milan fans or otherwise – will find that same joy. All told, it's not so suspect that the man who wrote this book supporters Inter.

Luigi Garlando

---

* Milan won the 1968/69 European Cup, their second in six years, beating Ajax 4-1 in the final in Madrid

THE FINAL – ACT ONE

European Cup final
Steaua Bucharest v AC Milan
Barcelona, May 24, 1989

During the eve-of-match team meeting, I open the newspaper and read the players a few lines of Gianni Brera's article. More or less, he says: "Milan are playing the masters of the dribble from the East. They must wait for them, trap them and hit them on the break."

Brera uses a term, *uccellare,* of which he is particularly fond. It's been explained to me as a neologism recovered from the Boccaccio era and derived from the French word *oiseleur*, which refers to the caging of small birds.

For the past two years I've been teaching the team to do the exact opposite, but still I ask them: "This is the advice that the most authoritative Italian sports journalist is giving us – should we listen to him?"

Ruud Gullit gets to his feet and responds: "Tomorrow, we attack them from the first minute for as long as we are able." Excellent. Two years of teaching is now enshrined in the heart.

The following day, it takes us almost an hour to make the short journey from our hotel to the Camp Nou. The Ramblas – and every other street – are a red-and-black tide, with 90,000 fans having come from all corners to support us. One hundred planes, 700 coaches, 5000 cars, even a boat: the biggest exodus in the history of football. Ceausescu's regime would not let the Steaua Bucharest fans out of Romania, and so all the tickets have ended up in Milan hands.

Our bus moves through the crowd at walking pace, like an icebreaker. Police on horseback struggle to open up the road by lashing out with their truncheons. The fans are shouting, singing, waving, slapping the sides of the bus. In her delirium, a girl opens her blouse and shows us everything.

Even Virdis, who always reads a book on the coach, is forced to look out the window – it's an unforgettable show. Baresi says to me: "Mister, who is going to explain to this lot if we lose?" I reply: "Franco – think only of us winning."

This is our game, our moment. We're better, stronger. We can't lose.

Somewhere in this sea of people are my Fusignano friends, who had set out in a minibus from the *Bar dei Repubblicani*. There's Alfredo Belletti, who taught me in school and about life. He arrived in Barcelona the day before the game with a toothbrush, toothpaste and a spare pair of pants in a Co-op plastic bag. He could only find a room at the luxurious Princess Sofia hotel, which cost him 650,000 lire a night (300 Euros today). His friends said to him: "Alfredo, dump your stuff and come with us to the Ramblas." His response: "You don't understand. To get my money's worth, I'm going straight to bed, and I don't even know if I'm coming to the game tomorrow."

Silvio Berlusconi joins us in the dressing room, deep in the bowels of the stadium. I tell him about our incredible bus journey. "You should have been on board with us, Mr President..."

He's obsessed with the facilities in the ground. I say to him: "Did you know that there's even a chapel down here?"

"Really? Where?"

He disappears, returns and tells me: "Arrigo, I prayed. And I told the Heavenly Father that the Steaua lot are all communists. He'll be on our side."

The boys are all sat staring at their boots, fully focused. There are only a few minutes until kick-off, and the weight of history and responsibility is suddenly making its presence felt. I walk round and pat each of them on the head.

We walk out. Seeing the stadium like that, absolutely packed to the rafters, sends shivers down your spine. It's just bank upon bank of people, all the way up into the sky. The whole world is watching us.

We're wearing our white change kit. I've given Ancelotti No.11 so that he seems a bit quicker. Evani has recovered from his injury but isn't yet in top condition, so I send out the same team that beat Real Madrid in the semi-final, with Carlo on the left flank. He was a bit worried about that move. I explained to him: "Don't worry, you'll always have two or three teammates around you, so you'll only have to cover a small space." With his game intelligence and perfect timing, I knew he wouldn't have any problems.

Maradona once said to me: "Even Ancelotti has become fast with you." I was moved to clarify: "He's not fast. He gets there first."

The referee, the German Tritschler, blows his whistle and we're underway against a backdrop of utter bedlam. They kick off but we're straight on top of them. We attack from the first second, just as Ruud had promised. We don't wait, we don't set traps.

I'm playing for the European Cup that I used to dream about as a kid sitting in front of Lorenzo Zagonari's television.

LORENZO ZAGONARI'S TELEVISION

Lorenzo Zagonari used to bank on the fact that it was his birthright to break – and that his opponent's hand would be shaky. He would thus optimistically bet one million lire per game. Pool: a Gorizia speciality.

Zagonari lost 18 games in a row – clearly his opponent's hand wasn't shaky after all. If you think that in 1968 my father had bought an apartment in Milano Marittima for six million, it's possible to deduce that Lorenzo had burned through three Riviera apartments in one fell swoop.

His opponent Galassi, who built the house in which I now live, was a real big-mouth. When Zagonari surrendered to the 18th defeat, he said: "Let's play again. I'm really not sure I'm better than you."

One of the factors in Fusignano moving from an agricultural economy to an industrial one was the fact that many sons of well-off land-owners, such as Lorenzo

Zagonari, had had a real good time of it and at a certain point came to the realisation that they would quickly devour their own inheritance if they didn't invest in something more productive. Lorenzo convinced his father to go into business and to sell four farming plots in order to buy a factory. In reality, he needed to sell two to cover his gaming debts and the other two to kick-off the industrial activity.

I've started this chapter with Lorenzo Zagonari because my long history with the European Cup all started in his house. It was in front of his television set that I began to fall in love with the style of football I'd adore my whole life, and I did it by feasting my eyes on the mythical Real Madrid.

In 1954, TV was still experimental. Only two families in Fusignano had a set, and one of these was Lorenzo Zagonari's. They lived a kilometre away from my house. I was eight years old, the World Cup was being played in Switzerland, and I was supporting Hungary – the kings of dribbling.

In the Romagna region at that time, there was a fierce rivalry between communists and Catholics. Deeply concerned, my mum asked me: "Why are you supporting Hungary? They're all communists there."

That summer I went on holiday to San Mauro Mare – between Cesenatico and Bellaria – with my aunt and uncle from Lecco. We stayed in Hotel Pieroni. One day, they couldn't find me; I had vanished into thin air.

My father had noticed that in one of the village bars there was a television set. "That's where he'll be," he said.

He was right. They had me sitting on a table, like a throne, in front of everyone. Uruguay were playing. I admired their athletic power and the grit of captain Obdulio Varela.

But my football was a different kind. I already loved teams

who set out to dominate and enchant through beauty, not force. Real Madrid, who won the first five European Cups, burst out of Lorenzo Zagonari's TV set with an irresistible charm. My eyes were wide open.

It was a true spectacle, a team full of all-time greats who always attacked and honoured the soul of football, a game that was born as an attacking pursuit and was then reduced to a defensive one. I don't remember much about the final against Fiorentina in 1957, but I recall the one where they beat the Milan of Juan Alberto Schiaffino and Nils Liedholm the following year.

Watching Alfredo Di Stefano really got me going: he had the gift of ubiquity. And then there was the Colonel, Ferenc Puskas. One day, I asked Di Stefano what he was like: "He was more dangerous 30m out from goal than a normal footballer is from five."

Gento played so wide that his real marker was the linesman. He'd play the ball forward, set off at a hundred miles per hour – uncatchable – and he'd even try to dribble the corner flag. Once I accompanied him on a visit to Milan. Lovely guy.

As a kid, I loved Real Madrid, Hungary and Brazil. A little later, I went mad for Ajax, because I understood that they'd taken a leap into the future. It was like when we won the European Cup and *L'Equipe* wrote, "After this Milan team, football won't be the same again". A new era had begun.

The Ajax show would make you dizzy. There was only one problem: it was almost impossible to follow what they were doing on TV, because the pictures were so tight. The Dutch wave spread far and wide, over the whole pitch. I risked falling off my seat because I leaned so far out in the hope of spying the part of the field you couldn't see on the screen. If I suffer from back pain today, it's partially the fault of that Ajax team who forced me to twist my neck.

Johan Cruyff was a fantastic player, pretty much without fault. A player is great if he plays with the team, for the team, anywhere on the pitch and the whole time. Cruyff was precisely that – he had everything.

Gullit, for example, did not know how to connect the lines of the team like Johan could, and for that reason I didn't play him as a No.10, for all he really wanted it. I preferred Donadoni in that role: he didn't score many goals but in that position he was the right piece of the puzzle.

When this Ajax pressed and lost the ball, the first to make his way back was Cruyff. He was the quickest and so saved his teammates the effort of turning round.

The players were great but so was the club. A true example. Ajax had two gentlemen coaches, Rinus Michels and Stefan Kovacs. When the Romanian Kovacs arrived, the Dutch – who, as I was to discover with Marco van Basten, are a bit stuck-up – began to mump and moan. Cruyff and Johan Neeskens, the captain, went to speak with the Ajax president, who asked them: "Have you got family problems? Has your car stopped working? Do you want to talk about your contracts? No? Well then, why are you here?"

"To talk about the team," they explained.

"I'm sorry, but you must only speak to your coach about those things. Good day, sirs."

The Dutch also honoured the soul of football: born as a team sport and then reduced to an individual one. That Ajax team played a football based on domination and beauty, they wanted to win on merit and they cared about values. Just as we would, later on.

There was one difference, however: they were more

concerned with the technical side of things, whereas we focused on movement. We were forced to do so. I only had Donadoni, Gullit and Van Basten who could beat a man with ease. Evani didn't always manage it and neither did Colombo, never mind Ancelotti with those battered legs of his. We had to create space with intelligent, collective movement.

I started coaching in 1973, right in the middle of the Dutch revolution. I was 27, and for some time it had been clear to me that I was never going to become a professional player. As a kid, I played on the wing, then as a holding midfielder, then full-back, then nowhere. A fairly inglorious procession. My friends called me Angelillo, but only because I was an Inter fan, just to be different from my older brother, Gilberto, who supported Milan.

Great forward, Angelillo. The year he scored 33 goals*, I saw him notch a marvellous one against Bologna. My father, who was from Mandello Lario, often took me to watch the Lecco team featuring Antonio Pasinato, Bengt Lindskog, Beniamino Di Giacomo, Sergio Clerici and Italo Galbiati, who would later work with me at Milan.

One time we went to watch Juventus in Vicenza. They were winning 1-0 when, in the 90th minute, Mario Maraschi hit a great shot from the edge of the box and, while the ball was in flight, the referee blew for the end of the game. The ball ended up in the top corner, and the stadium erupted in anger. That was the day I began to grow a little less fond of Juventus.

Father from Lecco, mother from Romagna – I'm the child of two contrasting cultures. From my father, a real

---

* Antonio Valentin Angelillo, an Italian Argentine forward, scored 33 league goals in season 1958/59, still a record for a single season in an 18-team Serie A

northern man with a rock-solid work ethic, I learned about the sense of duty and the absolute intransigence that's required when you take on a task. He had a share in two shoe factories and would leave the house at seven in the morning, returning only to eat his lunch. After dinner, he would go back to work until 2am.

I helped out with the Fusignano film club. The first movie we showed was *Battleship Potemkin*. When I started coaching, I never watched another film – it would have felt like I was stealing time from my work.

For 27 years, I gave football every part of me. Stress was a kind of added value, something that helped me grow, but in the long run it emptied me. In 2001, after a win in Verona with Parma, I realised I wasn't feeling any kind of joy. That's when I understood I didn't have anything left inside me and I stopped. It was a scare. I went to a psychiatrist and asked if that absence of emotion was normal. The response? "Your last 27 years have not been normal."

From my mother, Lucia, I inherited passion, energy and that touch of madness which is typical of the Romagna lands. Paolo Maldini called me a "visionary", which is a polite way of saying I was mad – exactly as Roberto Baggio did at the 1994 World Cup in America, tapping his forehead with his fingers.

Two mental hospitals were built in the area around Imola. It's said that the Romagnoli who live in that neck of the woods – Imola, Lugo and Fusignano – have felt the effects.

I believe that, to reach important goals, the necessary ingredients are dreams, a little bit of madness and above all lots and lots of hard work. I already had all of this in my blood, thanks to my dual soul. Gianni Brera once wrote about me: "Cross-breeds are the most dangerous of all."

My father was a good player. Paolo Mazza, who coached him at Portuense in Ferrara, where dad had gone to serve with the Siluranti regiment, subsequently took him to Spal. Years later, dad asked him to take a look at me, and so I too went on trial at Spal. Mazza confirmed himself as a refined connoisseur of football by ignoring me completely.

The first problem I had as a coach concerned a sweeper. I didn't have one. The director of second division Fusignano was Alfredo Belletti, my old Latin teacher and a former partisan. He was a librarian, host of the film club and a genius. He wrote a formidable tome about the history of our village that ran to 1226 pages. They stopped him, otherwise he would have gone on for more. "Fusignano has a population of 8000. If you wrote the history of Milan, you'd end up with an encyclopaedia," I always say to him. For 25 years, Belletti organised the Corelli Convention and had the likes of Claudio Abbado, Daniel Barenboim, Riccard Muti and the world's most prestigious conductors come to our village. Arcangelo Corelli, the master of Baroque music, was born in Fusignano.

I said to Belletti: "Alfredo, I need a sweeper."

"Ah right, and what number are you going to give him."

"No.6."

Belletti went into the dressing room and came back out with a No.6 shirt. "Here you go. And now, with ideas and hard work, go and make your own sweeper." In a heartbeat, he'd made me realise that there wasn't a single lira to spend.

Ideas and hard work. I had stopped believing in cunning and slyness when I was 10 years old. My father took me with him on a visit to clients abroad. We exported 90% of the shoes we produced – Germany, Austria, Holland…

Where I came from, people spoke of Germans as Krauts: hard, harsh people who were slow on the uptake, whereas we Italians were the cunning ones. On that trip, however, I noticed that the most low-level jobs were all done by Italians, Spanish or Turks whereas almost every German was going about in a Mercedes. I said to my dad, "Sorry, but weren't we meant to be the smart ones and them the dumb Krauts?"

And so, at the age of 10, I decided once and for all that cunning doesn't pay, and began to trust only ideas and hard work. I celebrated the European Cups won by the Grande Inter team as a fan, but without the joy and exaltation that the successes of Real Madrid and Ajax had given me. The reason? Inter won playing a style that had much more to do with cunning than with beauty.

When Helenio Herrera first arrived at Inter, he started out with a pure system: one centre-half, two full-backs, two deep-lying midfielders (Bruno Bolchi and Franco Zaglio, very attack-minded players), a right winger, a left winger, two inside forwards – one of whom was the self-same Angelillo – and the centre-forward Eddie Firmani.

In the first few games, Inter played courageous, spectacular football, winning and scoring a bunch of goals. I went to watch them away to Nereo Rocco's Padova, who had two merciless defenders in the shape of Aurelio Scagnellato and Ivano Blason. One laid you out and the other finished you off. In midfield, they had a really good Argentine, Humberto Rosa, and up there was Amos Mariani, a really quick right winger, and Sergio Brighenti, a combative centre-forward.

Inter went ahead after 10 minutes and continued to attack. Padova only got over the halfway line about five times, but scored twice and hit the post. The following day, Brera and the rest of the press got tore into poor Herrera, accusing him of being a *minus habens*, a naïve individual who didn't understand tactics. But what are tactics? They're about waiting for an opposition error in order to take advantage of it.

Herrera, who was a worldly man, said: "Ah, right. That's what you want? Ok, then that's what I'll give you."

That November, he bought Costanzo Balleri from Torino and played him 20 metres further back. Later on, he came up with the great idea of using Giacinto Facchetti as a full-back who defended by attacking. Giacinto was a marvellous player who would have been ideal for my Milan. He was two-footed, had a great shot and was excellent at heading the ball. He scored so many goals that Brera, at the peak of his exaltation, urged Herrera to play him up front. I was in the stand at Bologna when Facchetti played left wing. He didn't touch the ball. That was entirely logical. His strength was the perfect timing of his runs, as he showed in that brilliant 70m cavalcade which saw him score against Liverpool in the San Siro.

That Inter team won through individual prowess. In the 1964 European Cup final, Carlo Tagnin studied the photo of Di Stefano that Herrera had given him and then followed him round every inch of the pitch, even when he left it to have a drink. Herrera was no longer the sorcerer of his Barcelona days: he'd adapted and become Italianised, the exact same thing that would later happen to Sven-Goran Eriksson and just about every other foreign coach who arrives on these shores. They tried to normalise me as well, but they were not successful.

Like I said previously, I celebrated Inter's two European Cups as a fan, but without the enthusiasm of true admiration. I was already very demanding: I wanted courage, domination, beauty. The football of Real excited me much more than the triumphs of my Inter, and the same was true of the Benfica side beaten by Milan in the Wembley final of 1963. Jose Altafini reminded me of it not so long ago. "We were all back there, looking to hit on the counter-attack." Even after Benfica went down to 10 men 15 minutes into the second half after a bad tackle from Gino Pivatelli on Mario Coluna forced the playmaker off.

Three months after winning the European Cup, Pivatelli was coaching me at Baracca Lugo. On the few occasions he played me, as soon as I won the ball he would shout: "Pass it to Pollini! Pass it to Pollini! Pass it to Pollini!"

Once I asked him: "Excuse me, boss, but what do I do if Pollini is at home?"

How low must a player's self-esteem be if he is completely removed from the construction of the play? For this reason, in my teams I would always expect 11 players in an active position.

I went to watch Benfica against Juventus while I was doing my military service in Turin. I was a guard at the psychiatric wing of the hospital. A platoon of tramps, we were. At the morning 'present arms', there was one guy who would turn up in slippers, another in shorts. One day the captain got mad and ordered: "Nobody goes out tonight!" We'd normally be out and about in the city every night.

I simply could not miss the European Cup semi-final, the chance to experience live the emotion of the show that I loved most. I'd even gone to watch the training sessions of the two teams. I explained my predicament to the colonel, a Juventus fan, who said: "Don't worry, Arrigo. Swing by my house and I'll let you out from there."

Eusebio scored and Benfica completely dominated because Juventus kept Giancarlo Bercellino and Alberto Coramini all the way back and found themselves in constant inferiority against a team that looked to build through every single player. On one side, you had tactics – waiting for an opposition error. On the other side was strategy – a plan of action successfully carried out.

In 1988, 20 years after that Turin night, I stepped into the competition I had loved my whole life, since those days in front of Lorenzo Zagonari's TV. The most prestigious tournament, the one where Ballon d'Or winners are crowned and clubs get rich.

I would set about it with a hunger for domination and for beauty, the values that Real Madrid and Ajax had communicated to me. Strategy, not tactics. Using the strength of ideas and hard work, just as Alfredo – the Corellian librarian – had taught me. My Milan would not rely on cunning, because travelling around with my father selling shoes, I'd quickly learned that slyness does not pay.

The first time that president Silvio Berlusconi addressed me as the new coach of Milan, he tasked me with creating a team that could "conquer the world". I didn't point out to him that the previous year, Milan had finished only fifth and required a play-off to get into the UEFA Cup. Unlike the majority of people, I showed no scepticism when faced with the president's ambition. I felt myself lighting up with the thought that finally, after 15 years where the only thing people wanted from me was to avoid relegation, here was a real project.

I replied to Berlusconi: "Mr President, you and I both believe in the big dream. Now our task is to convince the team and turn our dream into a collective challenge."

But before we venture into the secret garden of the European Cup, we should recall how I ended up at Milan in the first place.

IN THE COURT OF BERLUSCONI

The first time I spoke to Silvio Berlusconi, he was wearing a short-sleeved shirt with narrow pinstripes. It was August 3, 1986. The pre-season friendly against his first Milan was a reward for my Parma side that had just come up to Serie B after winning the league.

The first half finished 0-0 and we were the better team. The previous season we had only conceded three goals at home: it wasn't easy to score against us.

In the second half, Milan's substitutions turned the tables and they won 2-0. The first goal came from Pietro Paolo Virdis, the second from Franco Baresi, who scored from the penalty spot two minutes before the end. We missed a penalty ourselves.

Berlusconi came down into the dressing rooms of the Tardini to offer his compliments and promised me: "I'll follow your progress." Speaking to the media, he added: "I really rate Sacchi, he's created an intelligent system. I'm happy to have given him Mario Bortolazzi, because he'll really be able to grow here."

But my satisfaction about our performance was stopped in its tracks by the serious injury suffered by Davide Zannoni, who ruptured knee ligaments in a challenge with Mauro Tassotti. Ginko Monti, the Milan doctor, only needed one glance: "He's knackered everything," he said.

I was really fond of that boy. I'd given him his debut in Serie C with Rimini. We'd left at the same time, him to Cagliari, where he didn't do well, and me to the Fiorentina youth set-up after Daniele Zoratto was sold against my wishes.

When I went back to Rimini a couple of years later, I re-signed Zannoni and he was top scorer in the division from a midfield role. I took him to Parma, where he was one of the key figures in our promotion to Serie B.

In addition to pain, there was anger because the Parma hospitals were running at minimal capacity due to the holiday period. We couldn't find anywhere for Davide to undergo immediate examination, and so he came back with us to our camp in Tizzano. Berlusconi heard about all this, and a few days later, together with his wishes for a speedy recovery, he sent Davide a Fiat Uno.

The Coppa Italia draw saw us end up in the same group as Milan. Exactly a month on from the friendly at the Tardini – September 3 – we went up against Nils Liedholm's team again, this time at the San Siro.

The previous day, my friend Giuseppe Nuvoli, a business and economics professional and one of the most fanatical Milan fans in Fusignano, said to me: "Arrigo, make sure and bring an umbrella, because tomorrow it will be raining goals."

I looked at him and replied, in total seriousness: "Beppe,

just to let you know that tomorrow I'm going to the San Siro to win."

The Parma president, Ernesto Ceresini, did not share my optimism. He saw it the same way as Giuseppe Nuvoli. He took me to one side and said: "Listen, Arrigo, we're right in the middle of our season ticket sales campaign. If Milan take five or six off us, we'll snuff out all the enthusiasm. Try to limit the damage."

After nine minutes, we went ahead through Davide Fontolan, a 20-year-old midfielder. Gianpiero Piovani was 18, Alessandro Melli 16. Milan could not catch us.

Riccardo Sogliano, the Parma sporting director, told me later that for the whole second half, president Ceresini had been grabbing his arm and saying: "Why doesn't Arrigo take off a striker? Why isn't he taking off a striker?" He wanted to bring home the result – he was thinking about season tickets. I *did* take off a striker, but to put another one on. And we still brought home the result. My bunch of kids had conquered the San Siro, and at the finish the crowd applauded us and jeered them.

In the press room, Adriano Galliani launched an appeal to the *rossoneri* fans: "We've given you so much, now we ask for a little patience." That summer, Milan had bought champions like Donadoni, Giuseppe Galderisi, Dario Bonetti and Daniele Massaro.

Once again, Silvio Berlusconi found me in the dressing room to offer his congratulations. "I'll keep an eye on you in the league as well. Finding the right motivation against Milan in the San Siro is easy. Let's see how you go against Serie B opposition week after week."

We won our Coppa Italia group, finishing ahead of the *rossoneri*, who everyone had tipped to enjoy a triumphant season. Not bad for a Parma team that had just come up from Serie C – Ceresini could be more than satisfied with his season ticket prospects.

Fate saw fit to pit me against Milan in the last 16 that same season, with the first leg at the San Siro. I remember the disappointment of poor Gianluca Signorini when he heard the draw. I asked him why he felt that way.

"Because I could already see myself as a grandfather, telling my grandkids about that time I won against Milan in the San Siro," he replied. "But if we lose badly this time, we'll ruin that first achievement as well. Miracles don't happen a second time, boss."

"Not always, Gianluca. But sometimes they do."

And on February 25, 1987, we beat Milan in their own back yard again. It finished 1-0 once more, but this time we scored at the end, through Bortolazzi in the 82nd minute. That night Berlusconi was probably a little less convinced that he had done the right thing in loaning him to us.

It was cold and the stadium was almost deserted: no more than 15,000 disappointed fans. Milan had been beaten again by a side just promoted to Serie B. By the return leg, a 0-0 draw that saw us qualify, Fabio Capello would already be in the hotseat. But at full-time in the San Siro, that great gentleman Nils Liedholm came to find me in the dressing room to offer congratulations and to shake my hand.

Berlusconi's words of praise came via the press: "Sacchi has built a likeable, sparkling side."

Speaking with those reporters, he admitted his concern about the move to allow a third foreigner, which seemed to be hanging in the balance. "We're in an awkward spot with Borghi," he said.

Milan had indeed already signed the Argentinos Juniors striker to play alongside Gullit and Van Basten the following season. Soon enough, Claudio Borghi would put me in an awkward spot myself. Less than a month later – I remember it well, it was the Friday before Messina v Parma on March 15 – I received a phone call from Ettore Rognoni. He is the son of Count Alberto Rognoni, the founding president of Cesena FC, editor of *Guerin Sportivo* and a great football man. Ettore, whom I'd known well for years, worked at Mediaset – Berlusconi's media company – and said: "He wants to see you on Monday."

I thought he wanted to talk to me about Fontolan, Melli and my other young players. Come the Monday, however, Ettore rang me back to say that the meeting would have to be postponed because Berlusconi's helicopter could not leave St Moritz on account of snow. The appointment was pushed back until the following week because that Wednesday and Thursday the president would be in Rome to finalise contracts with the television presenters Pippo Baudo and Raffaella Carrà.

"OK," I said. "But, to avoid any misunderstandings, if Berlusconi is minded to speak to me about becoming Milan manager, you should know that on Friday I'm meeting a Serie A club and there's a good chance we'll come to an agreement."

I didn't reveal the name of that club: Fiorentina.

A little while later Rognoni called again. "Are you busy tomorrow night?"

And so, on Tuesday evening, I came through the gates of the Villa San Martino in Arcore, a passenger in Ettore Rognoni's car. Silvio Berlusconi and Adriano Galliani were waiting for me.

I ate sitting directly opposite the president. We spoke about football from 8pm until 2.30 in the morning. I was struck by his passion, his enthusiasm, his cultured style. He made me feel at ease straight away. After only a few words, I had the strong, clear feeling that I'd known that man my whole life. I realised right from that first moment that we were cut from the same cloth; we were both born to dream big.

They asked me to postpone my meeting with the Serie A club and I agreed. But the following morning I had a re-think. Overnight, I'd been struck by a crisis of conscience. I called Ettore and explained: "I can't behave like this. On Friday, I'll go where I have to go to respect the commitment I've undertaken."

He tried to change my mind. "Are you mad? You can't throw away an opportunity like this! You're 90% of the way to being the new Milan manager!" I thanked him, but my mind was made up.

At that point, for me, the whole story with Milan was dead and buried forever. I wasn't thinking about it anymore.

I went to Parma to take the morning and afternoon training sessions. Back then, there were no mobile phones, and when I got back to the house, my wife told me that Ettore had rung four or five times.

I called him back and he asked: "Are you free tomorrow? I'm taking you back to Milan."

The following day, the Thursday, there was no Berlusconi. He was in Rome seeing Baudo and Carrà, but the whole Fininvest high command was on display: Berlusconi's brother Paolo, Galliani, Fedele Confalonieri, Giancarlo Foscale, Marcello Dell'Utri.

I was impressed by that line-up: it showed their stubborn desire to convince me and, indirectly, their faith in my work. I surrendered. "You're either madmen or geniuses," I concluded. "Give me the contract and I'll sign it even without a number for my salary."

To tell the truth, I did not expect that number to be less

than what I was on at Parma. Clearly these were some very intelligent madmen.

When the meeting was over, I immediately called Ranieri Pontello, the Fiorentina owner, to tell him I would no longer be meeting him because I'd just signed for another Serie A club. I didn't tell him which one, but I excused myself as best I could and offered my heart-felt thanks for the faith he had shown in me.

Pontello replied: "Look, Sacchi, if the club you've chosen is bigger and better than Fiorentina, I'm happy and won't have regrets. It will mean that I was right to be betting on you. But if it's a smaller club, I'll be sorry."

"I believe it's bigger," I replied. "Don't have any regrets."

So as not to waste any time, I introduced myself to the Milan players before I'd even seen them with my own eyes. I wrote them a letter with my best wishes for their break and outlined my founding principles as well as some tips for their rest period. This included a training programme that they would have to undertake before coming into our pre-season camp.

I told Vincenzo Pincolini, the fitness coach who had come with me: "Reduce the load by 20% on what we did at Parma, otherwise this lot will be scared off straight away."

Even so, I believe that when the players received the letter, most of them still suspected they had ended up in the hands of a madman. Or, at least, they were worried.

Here's what I wrote:

With this letter, I sincerely wish you a good break while also reminding you of a few behaviours and guidelines

which, if followed in this period of rest, will make the start of the pre-season camp easier for you.
In terms of training, my major hope is that nobody opts for too sedentary an approach. Especially up until July 10-12, a few games of tennis, a bit of swimming, walks and light jogging could happily resolve a lot of problems. In the last two weeks before our camp, it would certainly be better to follow a programme, even in a rough fashion. A programme with three sessions a week is attached herewith.
Provided they have been recommended by a doctor, sandbaths and thermal mud baths are another intelligent way of spending time on your break.
As far as rest and diet are concerned, good sense should be a more than useful guide. In addition, a good rule is to follow a slightly too heavy meal with more frugal, less rich ones.
Rest is very important. Always try to rest for at least eight hours, so that your holiday does not become a source of additional stress. A reminder that arriving in camp tired or even underweight would be the worst possible way to begin our activity.

This is the training programme I set out for the three weeks leading up to the camp:

First session of the week
10 minutes of stretching
15 minutes of continuous running
4 x five reps jumping, alternating between right and left foot
4 x 2 reps jumping, alternating between right and left foot

10 minutes of sit-ups
10x100m light running on the touchline,
gradually increasing the pace between 50-70%

Second session
10 minutes of stretching
6x20m skip (keeping the knees high)
3x50m (half a pitch) of alternating jumps
20 minutes of running at different speeds
(2 minutes slow followed by one minute faster)

Third session
10 minutes of stretching
10 minutes on abdominal muscles
6x10 reps of knee to chest
10x100m light running, gradually increasing the pace between 50-70%
15 minutes of running, gradually increasing the pace

By contrast, I went in a bit softer as far as the transfer market was concerned. Milan had already signed Gullit and Van Basten, two excellent players who up to then had only won trophies in Holland, except for the Cup Winners' Cup that Marco had claimed with Ajax when he had already been sold to Berlusconi.

I myself added three players who would prove fundamental to our era of success: Carlo Ancelotti, Angelo Colombo and Alberico 'Chicco' Evani.

Carletto's story is well known. I was in agreement with Galliani to sign him and Roma had agreed to sell him, convinced they were offloading on us a dud. Berlusconi – who knew all about the three meniscus and two cruciate ligament operations – wanted nothing to do with a player who was already certified as a 20% invalid.

I phoned him in St Moritz and said: "I'd be worried if the 20% was his head, but it's only his legs. We're lucky. I need a brain in the middle of the pitch." I then played my ace. "If you sign him for me, I'll win the league. Definitely."

Berlusconi signed him for me. I believe it was because I had shown the courage to dream.

Milan were in the process of selling to Udinese a central midfielder called Andrea Manzo, a good-looking lad who was seeing Dorina Vaccaroni, the Olympic fencer. I recommended that we include in the agreement Angelo Colombo, who had just gone down to Serie B with them, and we managed to do the deal.

I kept Chicco Evani, who had already packed his bags ahead of a move to Genoa. Liedholm had played him as a left-back but I had a different idea in mind.

I also brought in Roberto Mussi and Walter Bianchi from Parma, as well as Mario Bortolazzi, who was returning from his loan spell.

Milan were trying to sign Giovanni Francini from Torino for 6bn lire. "For 2bn, I'll get you two full-backs," I said, and this time my promise to Berlusconi was as follows: "I assure you that Mussi will play for Italy." When I became Azzurri manager and called him up, president Berlusconi rang me to say: "You were right. But it doesn't count."

Milan certainly could not accuse me of having demanded a lot in that summer market. They'd already signed Gullit and Van Basten. I'd brought in a central midfielder with one meniscus in four, a wide player who was just getting started, a defensive midfielder who had just been relegated and three kids coming up from Serie B. And all this to reinforce a team which had finished fifth the previous season. And yet, as I had learned right back at the start thanks to Alfredo Belletti, my old Latin teacher, ideas and hard work would decide my destiny much more than individual players. It had always been this way and it would be that way at Milan as well.

'Ideas' meant managing to communicate, in the quickest and clearest way possible, the principles of my football. 'Hard work' meant obtaining the highest levels of professionalism and effort both in training and in games, building a culture of generosity and sacrifice.

It was precisely for this second reason that I signed Walter Bianchi from Parma. I'd known him since our Cesena days, when I was in charge of the youth section and he was still playing with the kids, having not yet reached the reserve team. I remember seeing him one day wearing some battered old canvas shoes and a skimpy little jacket that was too tight on him.

It was snowing. I stopped him and asked politely, "Walter, what is your father's job?" He explained that he did not have a father, and that to support him and his two brothers, his mother – a janitor, but not with a permanent position – also did work in people's homes.

We had a bit of money put by at the club, and so we gave it to him. That very night, his mother called me, really concerned. "As soon as I saw all that money, I asked my son, 'what have you done, Walter?'"

I managed to reassure her. "Madam, your son earned it all. He hasn't done anything wrong." I also gave him two jackets.

Together with Bianchi at Cesena, I won the National Reserve League. I took him to Rimini, then he went to Brescia, where he didn't do well, so I took him back to Rimini. I brought him to Parma and then Milan. He was an extraordinary professional, a uniquely generous kid, always with a smile on his face.

That was the reason I summoned him to Milanello. I wanted my new players to see every day the level of professionalism it is possible to reach. Walter would be an example for them all, the embodiment of everything I wanted in their work.

I gave him his Serie A debut in our opening match against Pisa. He started with Mussi in the second game against Fiorentina. In two years, he made only three more league appearances, but he did his job to perfection. He gave us exactly what we wanted him to give. Walter Bianchi was a precious brick in the construction of my great Milan team.

SCUDETTO 88 – THE POWER OF THE PRESS

It was not easy to implement my way of working. Generally speaking, the players arrived 15 minutes before the start of the training session and, 20 minutes after it finished, they had already left Milanello. It annoyed me that they didn't stand up when president Berlusconi came to visit. For me, it was a question of good manners. We were in his home.

After the first few weeks, there were a few highly-charged arguments. Once, in the dressing room, I looked everyone in the eye and said: "I may well be a Mr Nobody, like the newspapers say, but in the last few years you lot haven't won much more than me. And if you continue to train as you are, you'll win even less going forward."

I was indeed a Mr Nobody, but I had been paying my dues for 14 years, from the eighth-tier Seconda Categoria right through to Serie B, without ever skipping a rung of the ladder or being fired. Not even at Alfonsine, where the previous five coaches had been hunted, and three of them beaten up.

I do need to make clear that none of the Milan players was prejudiced. I'd found guys like that in just about every other club, but not at Milan. If anything, they were sceptical, but never prejudiced.

One of the most sceptical, at the start, was Franco Baresi, but not because I gave him tapes of Signorini to study, as certain fantasists reported. That story probably arose from the Parma game that I showed everyone at Milanello, before our first league fixture. It was against Pisa, the Serie B champions whom Parma had beaten 2-0 in May. I showed the squad how we won the game – thanks, above all, to pressing. That lesson was for everyone, not just Baresi.

Naturally, I never gave Tassotti and Maldini tapes of Mussi and Bianchi to study. In fact, straight away I said to Mauro: "I've got loads of faith in you."

Tasso, a Roman with a quip always loaded in the barrel, replied: "Understood, boss. Otherwise you'd have signed four full-backs from Parma instead of two."

Truth be told, I'd arrived at Milan with the full intention of playing Paolo Maldini on the right, to take advantage of his stronger foot. But after a single practice match I changed my mind, and the Tassotti-Maldini full-back pairing soon became a permanent solution.

In the beginning, it wasn't easy to implement a new way of working and new behaviours, nor was it straightforward to get across new tactical ideas.

I don't like talking about revolutions. When people call me a revolutionary, I always like to point out: "The true revolutionaries are the rest of them. How did football begin? As a team game based on attack. Other people transformed it into a defensive, individualistic game. I'm the one who stays true to the origins. I'm the ultimate conservative."

Nonetheless, I was well aware that, in a culture so profoundly tied to Italian traditions, asking a team to defend by moving forwards and imposing collective pressing for 90 minutes, with 11 connected players at all times, did indeed sound like a revolution. This was the source of that initial scepticism from a few guys like Baresi and Van Basten, who were being asked to radically change the way they were used to acting on the pitch.

Pressing was the beam that held up the whole structure. As Costacurta admitted in an interview: "What did I think after Sacchi's first training session? This bloke will last two months."

The bet would succeed or fail right there in the quick and correct appreciation of an idea that, in reality, was simple: the closer to the opposition goal you win back the ball, the higher the chance of scoring. But to carry it out, the team needs to be organised and working in synergy – tight and compact. Always. Pressing done well saves energy: where you can manage a thousand little bursts per game, the number of 30m sprints you can do is much lower.

In that kind of system, a midfielder like Ancelotti – who had 20% lower capacity in his legs – could control the play quite happily, whereas he would have found it a lot harder had he been asked to cover large areas.

Pressing also boosts self-esteem because it makes you feel like you're involved even when you don't have the ball. Instead of controlling things, the opponent is obliged to do what you want, what you allow him to do. He has to move in response to your movements.

Every movement had to be synchronised and every player had to move in synchrony with his teammate. As an example, if Donadoni came off the right and moved to attack from a No.10 position, when we lost the ball, he didn't have to run the full diagonal to return to this original station. He would never have got there in time. He would retreat vertically into the midfield, a much shorter journey, like the one that Colombo would have carried out, moving horizontally to cover the flank left behind by Donadoni.

The zonal system is based on synchronisms, on men moving at the right time. Ten players in continual movement who are working to the same logic, bound by an invisible thread – the game.

With his tortoise formation, Julius Caesar taught us how important it is to stay compact in battle. He conquered Gaul with 50,000 soldiers. Keeping lots of players close to the ball offers two obvious advantages: when we're in possession, the ball carrier has more passing options; and when the other team is in possession, it's easier to get it back off them.

Plenty of critics tried to throw pressing back in my face as some kind of defensive fresh hell, when in fact it's the exact opposite. The quicker I win back the ball, the quicker I can attack, and even more importantly, the further from my goal I win it back, the less chance the opposition have of scoring.

Where I'm from, there's a saying: "If there's a gravedigger in your house, it means there's also a dead person." If you pull back and defend in your own penalty box, it's easy for the ball to end up in your net sooner or later. If, by contrast, you go and win it back in the opponents' box, it's more likely to end up in their net.

Over the years, I perfected the idea of pressing that I'd absorbed admiring the marvellous example of the Dutch, but I'd been aggressive from day one with Fusignano, down in the eighth tier.

The years I spent with the Cesena youths were a really important period of study that laid the groundwork for the experimentation I carried out with Rimini and Parma in the lower divisions. One Rimini game – against Modena – sticks in my mind. Gianluca Gaudenzi, who would sign for Milan in 1990, went in late on the right-back and laid him out. He then went in on the first central defender and laid him out as well. Still chasing the ball, he laid out the second centre-back, and when this third victim hit the floor, the crowd started to shout: "Stop! Stop!" He was truly possessed by pressing.

As soon as I arrived in Milan, I knew I'd reached the promised land, the ideal place to teach my football. In the early days, I'd drive to Piazzale Lotto and, while I waited for the bus to Milanello, I'd watch the people walking around about me. They all moved quickly, even the old folks. They were all in a hurry. The Milanese have pressing in their blood – trying to teach it in Rome would have been much more complicated.

To develop our pressing and intensity, I had a cage installed at Milanello. It was a mini pitch, 40m x 25m, with 2-3m high walls and a net on top. It felt like being inside the Sing Sing maximum security prison. Instead of doing 200m running drills, I organised three-minute training matches between teams made up of a goalkeeper and three outfield players. It was continuous aggression – the ball was always in play and never went out. I got hold of a ladder and I'd sit at the top, urging them on through a megaphone.

"I hear Arrigo doesn't shout anymore, he's got himself a megaphone," my wife said to Tassotti one day. "That's not strictly true," said Tasso. "Now he shouts into the megaphone."

I had to ensure they kept the energy high and got their

heart-rate to 160-170bpm, to make it a lactate workout with match intensity. We didn't have heart rate monitors in those days; we had to manually take the players' pulse. If it was between 110-120, I made them do running drills, so that in the next training matches they'd make more effort.

One day, the thing I ought to have expected did happen. Every three minutes the teams swapped over. Thirty seconds into the final match, a player was injured and had to stop. There was nobody to take his place, so I came down the ladder, laid my megaphone to one side and entered the field to fill the gap. The first time I had the ball at my feet, the three opposition players all slid in on me at once. If I hadn't jumped, I would have left behind my ankles, and maybe something more.

The actor Diego Abatantuono, a big Milan fan, came to train with us one time. It was his misfortune to arrive at Milanello when we were practising the press.

"How did it go?" the journalists asked him afterwards.

"Now I know how the ball feels in a pinball machine," he replied.

Ruud Gullit – a formidable athlete – was fundamental in both the honing and the application of the press. When he went hunting, he carried the whole team with him. He moved forward as irresistibly as a thunderstorm, covering the entire pitch. His power was incredible to witness – it seemed like opponents pulled back, scared.

Milan had bought him to be a sweeper. They'd seen him play that role for PSV Eindhoven in the Gamper Trophy in Barcelona. The Dutch viewed that role differently to us. They had a couple of markers, and then the sweeper had complete autonomy of movement. Ruud would launch these big 60m passes, and when he set off himself, he'd move up the pitch with incredible acceleration, as elegant as a sailing ship. Milan had fallen in love with him for these very reasons.

I, however, had seen him play really well on the right wing in a tournament in Utrecht, when I was coaching the Fiorentina youths. In the early days at Milan, that's where I played him, not least because I already had a sweeper, called Franco Baresi. But Ruud was fundamental above and beyond the tactical side of things.

Rijkaard had not yet arrived, and Van Basten had been out for ages. My whole first season at Milan, 1987/88, was down to Gullit. He wasn't the best technically – he had two pretty normal feet, and when we played games of foot-tennis at Milanello, everyone wanted to be on Christian Lantignotti's team, not Ruud's. But it was Gullit who made history, not Lantignotti, because game technique counts for much more than individual technique. In the middle of a match, in the middle of the team, Ruud's feet magically became the best, thanks to the intelligence with which he moved and linked with his teammates, which came through perfect management of space and time.

In addition, he had the charisma and personality of a great champion and made everyone feel stronger. He allowed the team to grow and to develop conviction. Ruud was our courage. In our very first league game, he put us 2-1 up against Pisa, and in all the key matches he was always a main man, including the famous head-to-head against Napoli in the San Paolo that saw us go ahead in the battle to win the league.

That debut goal against Pisa was a header that 50% of Italian players couldn't have matched for power with their feet. On the second weekend of the league season, we lost at home to a Fiorentina side featuring a young Roberto Baggio, who scored a spectacular goal. Van Basten criticised our play. It was too easy. He was a champion and me a Mr Nobody. The next day, there were headlines like: 'Van Basten deems Sacchi a failure; Van Basten attacks Sacchi' and so on. The following Sunday, away to Cesena, I kept Marco on the bench wearing No.16. I explained to him: "Seeing as how you know so much about football, you can give me some good advice from here."

He needed to understand that the club was in charge, and I was the club's man. There are two ways to establish authority: persuasion and percussion. Every now and then with Marco, I employed the latter.

In terms of character, Van Basten wasn't strong like Gullit, and he needed to be convinced of many things. For example, he was used to going deep and then coming short for the ball. As I explained to him: "Marco, in Italy it's better to do the opposite. Set off close to the ball and then attack the space in behind, otherwise you're making your heels too accessible."

In the fifth round of games, we went to the Marassi to play Sampdoria. Pietro Vierchowod went in hard on his Achilles heel and he was out for four months.

One day he came into my office at Milanello and left a note on my desk. He'd written, "Boss, today will you let us play a normal training match?"

He couldn't stand the themed games that I used to replicate match situations, coach pressing and correct the previous game's errors. If we'd hit too many long balls, I'd have us play practice matches keeping the ball on the ground. If we'd held onto it for too long, I'd put in a two-touch limit. If we hadn't had enough width, I'd make it obligatory to cross.

Van Basten would always say: "But boss, when we do it like this I can't improvise."

"That's not true, Marco," I would explain. "I'm simulating various game situations so that you can use the *right amount* of improvisation. You're not playing tennis; yours is a team sport. Let's say that improvisation tells you to dribble when there's a teammate free in front of goal, or to attack the near post when there's already a striker there."

Bertolt Brecht was right. "Without a script, there can be only improvisation and carelessness." It's just as true of football as it is of theatre.

I used to hammer Marco on pressing, showing him diagrams full of arrows. "See? When we lose the ball, if you go here and attack the opponent who's trying to move out, or here, where the pass might go, you stay in an active position, connected to your teammates. Those men are your strength. Otherwise, I'm a man down."

Brecht was right about this as well: "Even the most successful actors need other actors to be able to express their ability to the full."

One day, after a game, Berlusconi and Galliani came down to the dressing room to say hi. Angelo Colombo walked past and I congratulated him.

Galliani was taken aback. "But he didn't touch the ball!"

"Yes, but thanks to his movement, lots of his teammates were able to do important things."

Synergy was a founding value of that Milan team. Sharing an idea that allows the individual to get somewhere he would never have arrived on his own. Without those teammates, Van Basten would never have won the Ballon d'Or three times.

It wasn't easy at the start, and I wouldn't have succeeded had it not been for two very important interventions from Silvio Berlusconi. I enjoyed the same support from my president that Kovacs had found at Ajax. I too had become part of a truly great club. The first intervention came after our 2-0 defeat by Espanyol in Lecce on October 21, 1987 that ended up putting us out of the UEFA Cup. There was all sorts of criticism flying around and the papers were talking about me being sacked. Few people thought I'd make the turn of the year.

Berlusconi came into the dressing room and addressed the team in no uncertain terms. "We have faith in our coach. Those who share that faith may stay, the others can leave."

A true leader must speak like this: clear and concise. The following Sunday, the sixth round of fixtures, we won away to Verona and for the first time I began to glimpse my Milan. Having Evani fully fit again was a liberation: it allowed me to finally realise the ideas that were in my head.

I started out with a 4-3-3, the same formation I'd used with Parma. Ancelotti was on the right of the middle three – as he used to be at Roma – with Donadoni on the left and Bortolazzi in the middle. Up front, Gullit was on the right, Van Basten in the middle and on the left I'd alternate Virdis (the team's top scorer the previous season) and Massaro, who didn't really convince me.

Evani, returning from a serious injury, had always come on from the bench, but in Verona I started him in what would become the scudetto-winning foursome alongside Colombo, Ancelotti and Donadoni. Gullit was up front with Virdis, seeing as how we had lost Van Basten the week before at the Marassi. I had my 4-4-2.

On November 29, away to Empoli, even though we only drew 0-0, I was even more convinced, so much so that I declared post-match: "Today I saw the team that can win the league." One journalist remarked sarcastically: "Sacchi is the coach of the future, in the sense that he'll win the league in the year 2000." Instead, I won it within a few months.

The atmosphere around Milanello had changed. The players arrived much earlier and many of them stayed behind, voluntarily, at the end of the session to work on individual skills with Italo Galbiati. Nobody stayed seated when the president walked in.

One week, I reduced the training load because I thought the team looked tired. Franco Baresi came to tell me: "Boss, if we don't work on our defensive movements, we risk them no longer being second nature." Him, one of the most sceptical of all to begin with.

We really were on the right path – the challenge was becoming a collective one. As Ancelotti wrote in his book: "Arrigo was so convinced that in the end he convinced us all."

And yet, after our forfeit defeat by Roma*, which left us seventh in the table, the newspapers began to ask who would be Milan manager the following season. They took it as read that it would not be me. Berlusconi played the game and announced a press conference: "On Saturday morning, I'll reveal the name of the next Milan manager."

Journalists and TV crews filled the room with the hearth at Milanello, and the president, once more clear and concise, declared: "The next manager of Milan will be Arrigo Sacchi."

The previous time, he'd legitimised me and given me strength in front of the team, and now he was doing the same in front of the whole of Italy. The next weekend,

* Milan were handed a 2-0 defeat after Roma goalkeeper Franco Tancredi was hit on the head by a firework thrown by a Milan supporter called, somewhat ironically, Luigi Sacchi. Tancredi lost 30% of the hearing in his right ear as a result

we won the derby. When Riccardo Ferri's decisive own goal went in, I jumped so high that I tore my calf. It was December 20: I had made my first Milanese Christmas.

On January 3, we tore Napoli apart in what I still consider one of the best performances in our whole cycle. Careca scored straight away, but then we cut loose: Colombo, Virdis, Gullit, Donadoni, shots off the post and chances galore. Pressing and continuous attack for 90 minutes, with a quite crazy intensity. Gullit unstoppable. That day, Milan offered the first true picture of the football built on domination and beauty that I'd had in my head since childhood.

Van Basten was in the stand, having returned from treatment in Holland. He hadn't seen us play for a little while in the flesh and he was impressed. He told me: "Boss, I didn't believe that the team could change so much in four months." Another sceptic was being converted.

The following Sunday, we beat Juventus. We strung together five wins in a row and began to really put the heat on Napoli.

Van Basten returned to the fray in the 25th round of fixtures, against Empoli. He scored a brilliant goal, twirling like a swan. The following week, we won the derby with a performance that hit the same heights as the one against Napoli. The 2-0 final scoreline did not reflect our absolute domination. Inter couldn't manage to get out of their own box – as soon as they stuck their nose outside, we jumped on them. What a show. Gullit delivered another monstrous display.

For a full idea of what happened, the result tells less than a quip the Inter forward Spillo Altobelli made to the referee after half-time: "Count them properly this time. In the first half, there were 15 of them."

We were ready for the head-to-head with Napoli in the San Paolo. We attacked them from the off and went ahead through Virdis, but Maradona equalised with a free-kick at the end of the first half, which took the legs from under us. I went into the dressing room and saw everyone dejected, with their heads in their hands.

I stayed silent for seven minutes – as I always did – then announced: "I'm so sure we're going to win that I'm going to put on another attacker."

I took off Donadoni and introduced Van Basten alongside Virdis, who scored his and our second goal. Gullit went to No.10, the position he so loved but that I never let him play. Ruud had a brilliant game and Marco scored our third. We had accelerated past Napoli on the way to the scudetto.

The San Paolo applauded our beauty, confirming the extraordinary sporting culture of that crowd. Maradona – a big admirer of ours – also offered his congratulations. Later on, he tried to bring me to Naples. To convince me, he swore: "Boss, with me and Careca you'll always start out 1-0 up."

Diego was not the prototype of my ideal player. There were things that counted against him, but every rule has its exception. Had someone signed Maradona for me, I'd have gladly worked with him. He wasn't Borghi...

Milan – champions of Italy, at the first time of asking. Not bad for a Mr Nobody. I would be taking part in the European Cup, the trophy of my dreams. I immediately came up with two manoeuvres to attack it. First: a series of prestigious tests to take place between the end of the current season and the start of the following one. I had in mind a kind of European Cup of friendlies between clubs of noble tradition, to get my players used to the biggest games and grounds. Apart from the two Dutchmen, nobody had any experience in this regard. The second move was to request the signing of a world-class defender to help Baresi build our play. I'd already identified him. He was another Dutchman, who belonged to Sporting Lisbon but had spent the last year on loan to Real Zaragoza in Spain. His name was Frank Rijkaard.

The problem was that Milan had already signed their third foreigner, and Berlusconi had chosen him himself. It was the Argentine Claudio Borghi and it was a major problem. If I didn't resolve it, I wouldn't win the European Cup. That much was more than clear to me, but I had a strategy. Not a tactic, a strategy.

BORGHI OR RIJKAARD

I had discovered Rijkaard watching recordings of Van Basten. The summer I joined Milan, I watched Ajax's games to learn about the characteristics of my future centre-forward, and my attention was always drawn by that solid defender, who built the play with intelligence and often roared up the pitch himself. I kept an eye on him. The more I saw, the more I wanted him for my Milan.

I asked Gullit and Van Basten for information and both spoke about him with enthusiasm and warmth, not raising the slightest doubt. They had not been quite so generous with Aron Winter, whom they didn't deem of high quality, or Dennis Bergkamp, who did not, in their eyes, possess the heart of a lion.

As I was saying, the problem was that Milan had already bought their third foreigner (something that was allowed from season 1988/89). He was Claudio Borghi, the Argentinos Juniors striker, who had played against

Juventus in the Intercontinental Cup final in December 1985. Borghi's performance in that match – which was played in Tokyo – had made three presidents fall in love with him. They were Agnelli of Juventus, Berlusconi of Milan and Mantovani of Sampdoria. They all thought they were looking at the new Maradona whom Michel Platini had called "football's Picasso".

Berlusconi burned off the competition and a few months after Tokyo he had sealed the deal, initially leaving Borghi to play with Argentinos Juniors. The Italian borders remained closed to the third foreigner, and in the summer of 1987, when I joined Milan, Borghi went on loan to Como, where he did not manage to convince either Aldo Agroppi or Tarcisio Burgnich, who each had a turn at being manager that season and gave him seven appearances between them. During this difficult period, Berlusconi – with great sensitivity – called him often for a pep talk, urging him to stay strong and telling him he would soon arrive at Milan, where he would experience great things.

Borghi arrived at Milanello that April and started working with Pincolini, but it was as if he hadn't bothered. I can't remember if he did indeed ever ask me the question people say he did ("Boss, why run for so many miles when the pitch is only 100m long?") but he definitely could have. His work ethic was a long way short of ours.

Even further apart were our principles of play. I'll repeat: for me, a true player plays with and for the team, everywhere on the pitch at all times. Borghi played only for the ball. Of all the attributes and attitudes I look for in a player, he did not possess a single one.

I'd also taken a look at the statistics of this new Maradona. In 56 games, he had scored four goals. At his age, the old Maradona had already scored 260.

Regardless, that spring Borghi was already at Milanello and Berlusconi took it as read that he would be there the following season, too. I had already chosen Rijkaard and soon I'd have to speak to him about it. In the meantime, I got a promise out of him.

There were only a few games left in the league season, and Maradona's Napoli were still four points clear of us. At that point, it seemed crazy to think about overtaking them. Berlusconi was with Bettino Craxi, who became to some extent the guarantor of our bet.

"Mr President, if I win the league, you don't sign Borghi. Deal?"

To tell the truth, I'm not sure he ever said 'yes' but I definitely asked the question.

That May, we played the two glamour friendlies I'd arranged to celebrate winning the league, but above all to prepare the team for the forthcoming European Cup. The first was at Old Trafford on May 17, where we beat Manchester United 3-2. Borghi scored twice and produced a splendid assist from out wide for Van Basten to win the penalty which Virdis converted. Five minutes after his second goal, I took him off.

Naturally, Berlusconi had seen more than enough to satisfy him. After the game, he was radiant. "Arrigo, will you play Borghi from the start against Real Madrid as well?"

"No, Mr President," I quickly replied. "I need to rotate all the players."

Two days later, May 19, at the San Siro, Borghi came on in the second half with Real ahead thanks to a goal from Michel. The Argentine scored our equaliser, then Gullit netted the winner.

Like me, Adriano Galliani was ashen-faced. "What now?"

It was certainly a problem, because Galliani, who always

tried to help me in every way and who was an irreplaceable protagonist in all our successes, had already done a deal with Sporting Lisbon for Rijkaard. He had boxed him off, and I doubt Berlusconi even knew.

That wasn't all. I'd also sent Natale Bianchedi, my most trusted scout, to study Frank in Zaragoza for two weeks. I'd ordered: "Don't just watch him train. Watch how he behaves off the pitch, where and what he eats." For me, the judgement on the man has always been more important than the judgement on the player. Natale's report – like those of Gullit and Van Basten – was excellent. Frank was our man.

Galliani's conclusion, meanwhile: "This time, the president is going to sack all three of us."

On May 24, I flew with Ariedo Braida, our sporting director, to watch Holland v Bulgaria, a friendly before the European Championships in Germany. Rijkaard played in defence, just as I imagined him in my Milan. I wanted to field alongside Baresi another defender who could help him build the play. I wanted 11 players always in an active position, including the goalkeeper. Costacurta was never just a stopper, he always helped construct as well. In Italy, however, defenders aren't used to playing football, only to destroying it.

The football of every nation is dictated by its history and culture. We've only ever won one war, playing catenaccio on the Piave* then hitting on the break. Otherwise, we've always been on the receiving end and run away scared of this or that bully.

Spain, which ruled everywhere, has a much more ambitious footballing style as a consequence. The English

* The Battle of the Piave River was a decisive Italian victory over the Austro-Hungarian Empire during the First World War

style is courageous because they stood up for themselves even when the Germans were covering them in bombs.

The day after the Holland friendly, we went to Stuttgart to see the European Cup final between PSV Eindhoven, Gullit's old team, and Benfica, whom I'd seen in Turin while doing my military service.

Ariedo and I breathed in with some considerable pride the atmosphere of the most prestigious competition, which we would soon be taking part in. We couldn't possibly have imagined that in the very next final, our team would be out there on the pitch.

The game itself was disappointing, with two teams who sat back waiting, rather than trying to dare. The Dutch won on penalties. When we got back to the hotel, I had a message from Berlusconi's secretary. The president wanted to see me the following day. The moment of truth had arrived: Borghi or Rijkaard?

Berlusconi spoke first. "Dear Arrigo, just as I wasn't mistaken in betting on you, I'm sure I'm not wrong to bet on Borghi. I'm certain you will transform him into a true champion at the heart of a great Milan."

I replied: "Mr President, I consider myself first your friend and then your manager. Believe me: if we go with Borghi, we lose everything. Me, you and Milan. If you've chosen to keep him, I can't stay. For one simple reason: the team would stop following me. The players believed in my values and my football, and they followed me to the point of winning a totally unexpected scudetto.

"But Borghi does not possess a single one of those values, and so the players who have followed me up to now would be right to say: 'Boss, you've taken us for a ride this past year.' To be consistent, I can't stay. Carry on without me. But, I repeat, I'm your friend, and because of the debt of gratitude I owe you, I promise I won't go anywhere else: I won't take another job for at least a year."

A rest was what I needed.

In Serie B with Parma, I'd signed for only a year, announcing that I would quit coaching after that. I'd been thinking about it for three or four years, due to the stress – I had bad gastritis. But I'd then arrived at Milan and felt myself duty-bound to carry on for at least another year.

The tensions of life in Serie A, and a roller-coaster campaign between the initial risk of being sacked and the final triumph, had made my stomach even worse and we were now close to an ulcer.

Berlusconi tried again to convince me of Borghi's qualities, then said: "Fine. I'll get another coach, but you're staying as general manager for five years." The president never lets anyone go once they've won.

I replied: "Thank you, but after 15 years I'm not yet sure I know how to be a coach, never mind a general manager, something I've never done."

In the end, he surrendered and decided to keep me, not Borghi. Fedele Confalonieri remarked: "Sacchi, in my whole life I've never seen Berlusconi receive so many 'no's in one sitting."

It was May 26. Immediately after our meeting, the president flew to Ravenna to discuss buying the Standa chain of department stores with Raul Gardini. Carlo Sama, who I'd known since I was a kid – we even played football together – told me that Berlusconi said to Gardini: "Let's try to come to an agreement quickly. I've already got one Romagnolo busting my balls in Milan."

I couldn't give up without having at least one crack at the European Cup, the competition of my dreams, but when I went to see Galliani about my renewal, I asked for only a year. They wanted me to sign for three. In year one, I'd signed without agreeing to a specific salary. Now that I'd won the league, nobody could have any complaints when I asked for double.

Meanwhile, Galliani was awaiting the president's OK to fly to Lisbon to finalise the Rijkaard deal with Sporting. It was expected at 6pm, but instead arrived at 2am.

Adriano and Braida boarded a private jet bound for Portugal, and the following morning they were in the Sporting offices to sign the contract. But right in the middle of the meeting, the Sporting ultras, raging at the sale of Frank, broke down the door and started beating up the Portuguese directors. Galliani and Braida fled to a bathroom and locked themselves inside, along with the signed contract. Ariedo shoved it down his underpants. Having sneaked out of the offices, they informed Berlusconi of the mission's positive outcome. The president, scared by the tempestuous episode, advised them to get themselves to safety.

On June 15, I was in the stands in Dusseldorf for Holland v England, one of the group games at the European Championships. I was watching my three players, but I also kept an eye on Gary Lineker because, if Van Basten had not fully recovered from the previous season's injury, we would have looked to sign the English centre-forward. By the end of the match, that idea had already been superseded. Holland won 3-1 and Marco scored all their goals. The first was an absolute gem, with Gullit supplying the assist.

Full of enthusiasm, I immediately phoned Berlusconi to tell him what our centre-forward had done. He had a sensational tournament, finished off by that unforgettable goal against Russia: a right-foot volley almost from the corner flag, which put the Ballon d'Or in his back pocket.

Gullit and Rijkaard both played brilliantly as well, and they steered Holland to the title.

Having not won the European Cup for 20 years, Milan would give chase with three newly-minted European champions. And I was no less super-charged than them.

Claudio Borghi, after a short and sad parenthesis in Switzerland, resigned himself to going back to South America, where he finished off an anonymous career. He scored once for Argentina. He wasn't the new Maradona, after all. False alarm.

Instead, he became a good coach. With a certain irony, he was later called 'the new Sacchi' in his homeland.

Not long ago, Berlusconi asked me: "Would you take Borghi today?" I may have told him 'no' a ton of times back then, but he never gave up.

PRE-SEASON: MILAN MUST ATTACK

The team assembled at the Pala Trussardi indoor arena just as we had the year before. And just as had been the case 12 months previously, Silvio Berlusconi was absent. Coming off the back of a winning campaign, superstition made people want to stick to the same script.

Cesare Cadeo, a lovely, passionate man who sadly passed away in 2019, presented the new season's Milan to 10,000 enthusiastic fans who chanted "Champions! Champions!"

There was an incredible crowd, despite the fact it was a horrendously hot summer Saturday and the city was deserted. It was July 23. A five-year-old girl gifted me a red and black bracelet.

Other big teams were getting together that day, too. *Gazzetta dello Sport* published a front page comparison, and for us it was a walkover. Three thousand people had gathered to welcome Inter, 1000 for Juventus. I've always been as proud of this type of statistic – increasing the number of people who follow my teams – as of the trophies we won.

There were 30 spectators when I started out with Fusignano. When I left, the number was 400. The same thing happened at Bellaria, Rimini and Parma. When I first arrived at Milan, we had 30,000 season ticket holders. The following year, we had 60,000. That's why we are involved in football – to entertain people. Winning will never be the only thing that counts.

One day Marco van Basten said to me: "Boss, we're working too hard. I'm not enjoying myself." I explained to him: "Marco, I've never seen anyone reach important objectives without working hard. And in any case, you should enjoy seeing how much fun the fans are having thanks to our hard work."

After the event, we had lunch at the Ribot restaurant close to the San Siro racecourse, where I posed for photos with the three Dutch players and chatted with the journalists. I put my cards on the table straight away. "Remember that the last time Milan won two consecutive titles was 80 years ago." And I reminded them where we'd started from. "If I'd said to you this time last year that we'd win the league with a midfield four of Colombo, Ancelotti, Donadoni and Evani, you'd have called me mad."

The reporters asked Rijkaard if he knew who Gianni Rivera was, hoping to catch him out as they had with Gullit. But we'd got him well-informed and he said he'd watched him as a kid in the 1969 European Cup final against Ajax.

Frank was the big new face of our season – pretty much the only new face, in fact. The rest were the ones who had won the league, apart from Fabio Viviani – signed from Como – and two reserve goalkeepers, Davide Pinato and

Francesco Antonioli. We took both because we didn't know which one to choose.

That afternoon, we went up to Milanello, where Father Massimo Camisasca blessed us, and we undertook our first training session, led by Pincolini, the fitness coach. I had injured myself playing in a training match at the seaside with Bagni and Cabrini.

The following day, there was a tornado at Milanello which saw the supporters flee, but we kept training regardless. Throughout ancient history, major achievements were often heralded by special atmospheric events.

One night I watched recordings of a couple of our matches with Rijkaard. They were our 4-1 win over Napoli, the one where Van Basten had held court, and the 2-0 win over Inter that had left Altobelli so shocked. Our two best performances of the previous campaign. Frank was enchanted by two players in particular: Gullit and Ancelotti. He said: "Your pressing is excellent – I'll have fun. I've never seen Ruud run so much without the ball in Holland. But sorry, why have you signed me when you've already got a professor in midfield?"

He was talking about Ancelotti. Like I said, I wanted to play him in defence, to increase the quality of our build-up play. I should be clear – I was more than happy with my defenders. In the league the previous year, we had conceded 14 goals, two of which were in forfeit, so only 12 on the pitch. Almost half the number from the year before.

The players were the same – in fact, I played Filippo Galli, who under Leidholm had been deputy to Dario Bonetti, a first-pick in the national team. The difference was that now, we defended and attacked all together.

Rijkaard could give me more quality constructing play from the back, but I immediately noticed that he played the role in a very Dutch style, caring more about the physical duel with the opponent than being in synchrony with his teammates. For me, a player's hierarchy of interests must be: teammate, ball and in last place, opponent. For the Dutch, by contrast, hand-to-hand combat is the priority. The problem here is that the team struggles to move as a single organism.

It didn't just happen to the Dutch. If I almost never called up defenders like Beppe Bergomi and Ciro Ferrara to my Italy squads, it was precisely for this reason: their reference point was more the opponent than their teammates. I often showed my defenders four fingers of an open hand, keeping my thumb flat against the palm. "You are the fingers of one hand. See? The ball can pass between one finger and the next, but if I close them, it can't get through anymore. And it can't get through if one fingers moves up to have a go and the other three close ranks on his shoulder."

In the midfield, meanwhile, Rijkaard would become one of the main reasons the whole organism flourished. He was the perfect balancer, who dictated our timings and ruled the space. He was a precious asset in both covering the defence and supporting the attack, and would score decisive goals. He was the complete player – an encyclopaedia.

Right from the first pre-season friendly, away to Brescia on July 31, he made a huge impression on everyone through his personality and control. Berlusconi told the journalists: "He's the player we were missing."

That's right: him, not Borghi.

We did, however, lose that friendly 2-1, partly because I picked only a few of our regular starters but mostly because that morning I'd absolutely killed them in training, as is made clear by the session plan from my diary shown in these very pages:

11 v 0 match. Team exercise to fine-tune the co-ordinated movement of each player
Continuous running
10 minutes of skipping and explosive starts
5 minutes of hurdles
5 minutes of 9 v 9 in the cage
10 minutes of full-pitch game, 11 v 11, with drills on pressing, zonal work, quick counter-attacks, free-kicks and corners
15 minutes of 2 x 1200m, at a speed of 4min 30sec per km, 2min 30sec rest
Uphill running

To be fair, that evening when it came to the game, they had every right to be tired.

I made a note of everything we did, day by day, in a Smemoranda diary that was bigger than the usual type. The 1988 diary had a grey cover and pages made up of little squares. I kept my writing really small so as to fit in as much information and as many reflections as possible. I recorded the type of drills we did and the training load of each session. I drew little diagrams of the moves we'd tried and I rated the effort of the players.

For the games, meanwhile, I wrote a comment, noting the things that had worked best and those which we needed to work on. I passed judgement on the players and sometimes gave them a mark.

I didn't always write in a diary format and I often used the second person, because the things I wrote then became a discussion in the dressing room. In front of the team, I would read out even the harshest comments. In fact, *especially* the harshest comments, to give them a shake and provoke a reaction. Each pad, which I keep like treasure in my study, is the black box of a season, the story of our work and our feelings. They show how my Milan flew that year, day after day.

After defeat in Brescia, I wrote:

> *We took a dive into our new reality. The time for celebration is over. This year, everyone will look to take us down. But Milan must attack, not be attacked.*

I then noted the things to improve:

> *Pressing, speed, shaking off markers, both individually and collectively.*

That collective work to shake off markers did the players' heads in. If one came across from the left, the other had to move across from the right. If one attacker came short, the other should go long. I expected everyone to stay active, even when they didn't have the ball: with their movement, they could create space and possibilities. I hammered home this point like a madman, especially at the start.

Another note from Brescia:

> *Improve our capacity for making judgements, for example when to hit the ball long or carry it.*

I always said to Baresi: "Franco, you should know that every time you hit the ball long, it makes me sad." I wanted the ball to move forward via a pure team harmony.

I also wrote: *Player rotation is necessary, even if it ends up making us look bad.*

That's exactly what happened in our first outing, but my job was to think about Vitosha (now Levski) Sofia, our first opponents in the European Cup.

The newspapers spoke about a "trick", because I'd left out a lot of usual starters. They criticised us heavily, to the point where I wrote in my diary: *Media: over the top reaction.*

In one sense, it was easy to understand. Many of them had eaten humble pie the previous year, and they couldn't believe we had lost our very first match this time round.

I tried to calm them down: "I'm not Don Quixote. We'll give a truer account of ourselves in Parma."

In reality, we didn't do well there either, not least because that morning Pinco tortured them with uphill sprints for two hours.

Parma was where I'd met Vincenzo Pincolini. I'd never had a fitness coach before – I'd always taken care of that aspect myself. Only in the first year at Rimini did I have some help from Paolo Baffoni, who would later work with Alberto Zaccheroni at Milan.

When I returned to Rimini, I had the support of a coach whose job was to look after the rehabilitation of injured players. When I got to Parma, I said: "I don't need a fitness coach – I'll do it."

Riccardo Sogliano, the sporting director, replied: "As you wish. But we have a good one. Use him if you want to."

After a single week, I realised that Pinco knew 10 times what I knew. Because he was a school teacher, he wavered for some time before following me to Milan.

"Some faith you have in me, Vincenzo," I said to him. But I understood. I'd explained to him that I would only be signing for a year at Milan, because my intention was to stop coaching. Quite rightly, he thought twice before leaving a secure job. Eventually, he decided to take a leave of absence from teaching, and he followed me to Milan. We won the league and he carried on as fitness coach. He was the father of that profession, a master, an authority, a friend.

The Parma friendly finished 1-1 and on August 7 in Verona, it went even worse: we lost 1-0 to a goal from Pedro Troglio. Verona always did bring me bad luck.

In my logbook, I wrote:

> *Ugly game. Slight improvement in our effort, but team looked stretched and intensity was low. We're not marking enough and we're slow.*

I could well believe it, looking at the session plan from that morning:

> 10 minutes of 11 v 0
> 10 minutes of a handball training game, 8 v 8 on a 30x40m pitch (*We did this because the real problem is never technical but one of ideas and correct movement. If you move out when you should be going narrow, you do it with your hands as well as your feet)*
> 10 minutes in the cage, pressing drill, 6 v 6

Ten minutes of continuously attacking a ball that doesn't go out is a never-ending hell. As if that wasn't enough, we kept the *coup de grace* for the very end of the session: 6 x 100m sprints, 10 times over. Quite the nice little programme.

The media, who didn't know our training loads, judged us purely on results and performances. Their criticism was getting more robust and the general worry became more widespread. At the end of the day, we were exactly a month away from our debut in the European Cup.

Berlusconi could tell which way the wind was blowing. He called me from Bermuda and said: "Take no notice, Arrigo. Keep working away calmly and follow your own path."

In reality, those friendlies were only staging posts on the way to the more important matches of our pre-season that I'd scheduled with an eye on the European Cup. I wanted to get us used to that environment through international tests against clubs with great history and tradition.

It was also the case that Serie A that year would not start until October 19 because of the Olympics in Seoul, and as such I couldn't count on competitive games – always more psychologically important – to prepare for our continental bow against Vitosha Sofia on September 7.

In the space of a few days, between August 13 and 17, we played Bayern Munich, Tottenham Hotspur and PSV Eindhoven – the reigning European champions. And on September 1, we paid a visit to Real Madrid in their own backyard for the Bernabeu Trophy.

We started out on August 13 against Bayern Munich in the Wembley International Trophy, on the same pitch where, a quarter of a century previously, Milan had won their first European Cup. For us, keen as we were to connect the club's glorious past to the present, that experience was along the lines of a Voodoo ritual.

We won 1-0, thanks to a goal from Virdis. Van Basten could have rubbed it in, but missed an extraordinary chance. Afterwards, he excused himself as only he could: "I don't like to make people cry."

We played really well, and the English journalists were all over me to understand how. I tried to explain: "Yes, we're Italian, but we play to bring enjoyment."

What a satisfaction: the English crowd applauded us, they

understood it perfectly. Europe was beginning to discover that we were here to tell a completely different story.

In my logbook, I wrote:

> *Good game, excellent organisation. Good individual displays from everyone. A great experience. Things to improve.*

That was my strategy. When the team had done well, and was thus more optimistic and receptive, that was the time for me to insist on the things we needed to get better at.

> *Finishing, assists, rapid counter-attacks, one-twos, one staying and one going, players criss-crossing to switch position.*

The following day, we beat Tottenham 2-1 with goals from Virdis and Van Basten. I still wasn't able to field Gullit, who was injured. Riding a wave of enthusiasm, I announced to the media: "This will be Marco van Basten's season."

I phoned Berlusconi, and even before relaying the result, I told him: "Mr President, we again left Wembley with applause ringing in our ears." Like me, he wasn't interested in a win without merit, without values or without beauty.

> *Good game, strong team, our future can become excellent.*

On the page for August 17, PSV Eindhoven v Milan, I wrote a bit more:

> *Good first half: Pressing, offside and zonal marking.*

Good and efficient counter-attacks. Good organisation, on an individual level, good performances from everyone apart from Costacurta, Colombo and Virdis. Second half not great, team stretched and not very organised, pressing non-existent.

I was always banging on about pressing. It was the key to everything.

Few switches of position, and those that we did were wrong. Poor marking.

Then came the homework:

Mussi: one-twos, headers and shots. Costacurta: work on offsides, zonal marking and long balls. Rijkaard: finishing. Donadoni: positional switches and finishing Van Basten: positioning for pressing

PSV were reigning European champions and had not lost at home for eight years. Rijkaard, who started out at Ajax and enjoyed the win more than most, continued to repeat that fact in all his interviews. In the Dutch papers, we saw the headline: 'A footballing lesson.'

Gullit missed that match as well, and in the following weeks his absences, his troubled start to the season, became a bit of a *cause celebre*. He had little knocks and ailments in his ankles and knees, but the bottom line was that in his first year, not even a train could take him down, whereas in his second, all it took was a breath of wind. The smallest pain was enough to stop him. He spent too much time thinking about women and he was always injured.

That first year, I'd only had one real harsh verbal exchange with Ruud. He had come back from a Holland match on the Thursday and trained well. I breathed a sigh of relief because usually when players returned home to play for their countries, they found a way to enjoy themselves. Ruud trained well on the Friday too, but on the Saturday morning, his wife called me asking about his whereabouts because he'd been out all night. When he turned up at Milanello, he looked like a ghost.

After the morning session, we left for Avellino. As we were getting on the plane at Malpensa airport, Ramaccioni whispered to me: "Arrigo, Ruud is missing."

I said to Baresi and Ancelotti: "Go and get Gullit – I bet he's fallen asleep in the departure lounge." Sure enough he had.

Once we got to Avellino, I called him to my room and gave him the full hairdryer. "Are you not ashamed? Have you not looked in the mirror? It's the first time I've ever seen a black man turn white. You look like a ghost. You're thinking with your dick, not with your brain." Those were my exact words.

The following day, he was like a pole, stuck in the ground as the game continued around him. We drew 0-0 with Avellino. A few weeks later, Gullit had that great derby, one of his best-ever performances. After the game, he asked to speak with me.

"Boss, that time before Avellino I made a mistake and I'm sorry. But if you ever have reason to tell me off in future, don't bring the colour of my skin into it again."

Every player, every man, has his own sensibilities, his own character. A coach must know which buttons to press and which not to. He must understand whether that player can be criticised in public or if it's better to do it in private so as not to wound his pride. Once, during a training session,

I went over the top in scolding Mussi and I made him cry.

In the first Coppa Italia match against Licata, Carlo Ancelotti – a man who has known true pain – hurt his knee again. A real blow. They immediately operated on his meniscus.

On September 1, we stepped out at the temple of the Bernabeu, kingdom of the great champions who had opened my eyes as a kid. Home of the mythical Real Madrid who had won the first five European Cups. On this evocative journey towards our debut in the most prestigious continental competition it was obligatory for us to stop off there, otherwise the voodoo would not have worked to perfection.

We were missing Van Basten, but we won 3-0 with goals from Donadoni, Mannari and Maldini. It was the Bernabeu's turn to get on its feet and applaud us.

Luisito Suarez, the legendary Ballon d'Or-winning Barcelona and Inter forward, came looking for me to offer his congratulations. He was enchanted. "Your Milan team can win the European Cup because it thinks big!"

Overcome with emotion, I thanked him and said: "Do you know that when every Juventus fan in Romagna was going mad for Omar Sivori, I was your No.1 supporter?"

Not so much because I was an Inter fan, but because when Sivori played, he watched the ball, whereas Suarez watched his teammates. Luisito, when he had the ball at his feet, thought big as well.

Berlusconi, in ecstasy, told the journalists: "Sitting beside the Real president, Ramon Mendoza, I wasn't even able to celebrate. But as soon as I get home, I'll be doing pirouettes. We've put three goals past Real Madrid in their own backyard!"

Speaking to me, he added: "Arrigo, tonight five million

people were watching us on TV!"

This was the real source of his pride: that Milan were becoming a show for everyone, something that entertained people. That meant he could sell it at a good price to be shown on prime time TV, but much more important to him than the money was the satisfaction of the businessman who, thanks to ideas and hard work, was building something beautiful, something that could conquer the world.

Gullit supplied the dressing-room champagne to celebrate his 26th birthday, while updating his list of knocks and niggles. He promised he would do everything in his power to be there in Sofia, against Vitosha, one week later.

By now, it was becoming hard to keep ourselves a secret.

Everyone had noticed what we'd done between the end of the previous season and the start of the current one. In six glamour friendlies, we'd beaten Real Madrid twice, as well as Manchester United, Bayern Munich, Tottenham and PSV Eindohoven, the reigning European champions. The voodoo had worked perfectly.

As the predictions began to come thick and fast and many attached the label of favourites to us, I tried to keep my feet on the ground: "It's true that we've beaten big teams, but it's also true that we've lost to Brescia and Verona."

I went a bit over the top. At the Bernabeu I let myself say: "We played really well against Real Madrid, but I was more worried before our first Coppa Italia match against Licata."

Even in my logbook, I was urging caution: *The players were good. Margin of victory excessive.*

However much I tried to put the brakes on, I felt we were ready to climb the great mountain, despite our absentees and inexperience in the competition. Only the three Dutch players had ever set foot there before, and they'd only gone a short way. The first step on the great mountain was called Vitosha Sofia.

COLOMBO'S BUTLER

European Cup
First round, first leg
Vitosha Sofia 0 Milan 2

The day before we made our European Cup debut against Vitosha, Silvio Berlusconi came to our team hotel in Sofia. It was the afternoon, and I was asleep. That in itself was strange because I usually never took a nap after lunch, plus I had several reasons to be losing, rather than gaining sleep, at least in the afternoon. For example, there was the emotion of taking my first steps in the competition that I'd dreamed about since I was a kid, and the absence of three of the team's pillars, one per department: Baresi, Ancelotti, Gullit.

However, the summer friendlies against prestigious clubs had given me a great sense of calm – they'd been the confirmation that the team had assimilated the principles of our game really well. And when you have a game, you can sleep well, even when you're missing players.

Perhaps the three Vitosha spies who had watched us

score three times against Real Madrid were not quite so serene. "And that was without Van Basten," they kept reminding one another.

After being woken up, I came downstairs to say hello to Berlusconi, who greeted me with a smile. "Just like the Prince of Conde*, sleeping before the battle!" And just like the French at Rocroi, we won, in the exact manner that Gullit had predicted when chatting with the media the day before the game.

"My teammates will score in the first half, then I'll come on to finish the job." Virdis did indeed score, in the 18th minute. In the 70th minute, he was replaced by Ruud, who took only five minutes to find the back of the net.

We dominated from start to finish, much more than the scoreline suggests. The Bulgarians were completely taken aback by our pressing. Costacurta – a 22-year-old kid – proved an able replacement for Franco Baresi, while Rijkaard, the best player on the pitch, gave a stupendous performance.

Vasil Metodiev, the Vitosha coach, was impressed by Colombo's display, to the extent that in the post-match press conference he said he was his man of the match. In addition to being one of the key figures in the pressing that ultimately won us the game, Angelo had delivered the crosses for both goals.

One day, the 1982 World Cup winner Ciccio Graziani, asked me: "What have you done with that lad? When he played with me at Udinese, if I went to the near post, he crossed to the far post. If I went to the far post, he crossed

---

* In Alessandro Manzoni's *Promessi Sposi* (The Betrothed), a seminal work in Italian fiction, he recalls how the Prince of Conde always slept well before battle, because he was so sure of his planning and strategy

to the near post. If I went to both of them, he'd hit the ball straight out."

We hadn't done anything with Angelo, truth be told. He'd done it all himself, through his desire to get better and his willingness to make sacrifices. Every single day, he would stay behind to do technical drills with Italo Galbiati and, in time, even his crosses began to end up in the right place. Ideas and hard work – that's what it always comes back to.

Galbiati was an important figure. He didn't just have an influence on the pitch – he would talk to the players and smooth over the most spiky of situations; a true diplomat, experienced and full of good sense. That Milan would not have existed had we not become a team off the field as well; had we not shared the same idea. From president Berlusconi to the people working in the kit store, everyone played their part to perfection. The doctors, Giovanni Battista Monti and Rodolfo Tavana; the psychologist, whom I needed more than the players; Paolo Taveggia, the team manager; poor old Guido Susini, the head of communications. Plus, naturally, Adriano Galliani, one of the best directors in the history of world football. Passionate, brilliant, never intrusive, even though he knew the game inside out.

I remember Tokyo and the scenes after Evani's last-minute goal in the Intercontinental Cup final against Medellin. I saw a man in an overcoat come onto the field and run to the centre circle. I thought it was a pitch invader – nope, it was Galliani.

Angelo Colombo was a key piece on my Milan chessboard. He never tired of running and he did it very intelligently: he knew where and how to run, even without the ball. He gave crucial help to the defence, and was just as precious in our attack. Thanks to the way he covered and the way he moved in space, his more technically gifted teammates could express the best of themselves. For this reason, in the dressing room you'd often hear a chant of: "Fly, Colombo, Fly!"

When Real Madrid were celebrating their centenary, they gave me the task of putting together and coaching a Rest of the World select. As soon as I ran into Rafael Gordillo, the left-back who always came up against him on the flank, I told him: "I've brought Colombo." The colour instantly drained from his cheeks. "No, no, I've had quite enough of Colombo!" What battles when those two great runners went head-to-head.

Angelo Colombo was not an absolute talent. He wasn't the sort of star player who you can rely upon to boost prime-time ratings. Indeed, at the time when Borghi's arrival was being discussed, Berlusconi threw that back in my face: "I haven't spent 100 billion [Lire] to watch Colombo play!"

My reply? "As long as I'm manager, whoever deserves to play, will play."

In time, though, the president probably understood that it was the team who needed to shine on prime-time TV, not individual players, and that Colombo was just as big a contributor to Milan's beauty as anyone else. Indeed, when I told him in 1990 that we needed to sell Angelo, Berlusconi tried to change my mind.

I'd called Colombo to my office and spoken clearly to him. "Angelo, this isn't good enough. With this level of effort and these returns, you can't stay at Milan."

With huge honesty, Angelo replied: "Boss, I've gone beyond my wildest dreams. I'm drained. You're right – I'm no longer managing to give what I did before. I don't have the same motivation."

I told Berlusconi, who wanted us to take our time. "Let's

wait and give him a few months. Maybe he'll get back to his old ways. He's always been important for us."

A couple of months later, I went to see the president again. "I'm sorry, but nothing's changed. We need to sell Colombo."

Once more, Berlusconi sought to mediate. I stopped him and said: "Define Angelo Colombo."

The president thought for a moment, then reached for a cycling term: "He's a *domestique*."

"Quite," I replied. "Well, I phoned Angelo's house one day and it was the butler who responded, saying, 'the master is not home'. Have you ever heard of a *domestique* with a butler?"

Berlusconi agreed to the sale, and it earned him some decent money from Bari. For the sake of honesty, I told Gaetano Salvemini – the Bari coach at the time – how it had gone with Angelo, but they still wanted to give him a two-year contract worth 750m Lire per season.

Our debut had gone well. I'd won my first match in the European Cup, but judging by the calmly scientific comments in my log-book, I didn't get too excited.

> *Good result. A good match defensively but only just good enough in attack. To be improved: the collective shaking off of markers, and our cover movements.*

Berlusconi seemed much more excited than I was, opting for a metaphor inspired by one of his favourite passions: "We've started pulling on the skirt of Europe. Let's hope we're looking her in the eyes before long."

At that point, the second leg at the San Siro appeared to be a formality, but a series of unfortunate coincidences changed the picture quite incredibly.

First of all, four of my men were called up by the motherland for the Seoul Olympics: Colombo, Tassotti, Evani and Virdis – half the starting team.

Then, on September 20 during a training session, Gullit collapsed to the ground, screaming, with nobody near him. He'd twisted his ankle and would be in plaster for a month. Ancelotti was still out, Costacurta and Maldini had problems too, and Van Basten had gone back to Holland for treatment. To call it an emergency would have been an understatement.

Indeed, on September 21, in the neutral surrounds of Bergamo with a team full of youngsters, we couldn't manage more than a draw with Osvaldo Bagnoli's Verona. Claudio Caniggia put them ahead and then Baresi equalised.

On September 29 we lost 1-0 to Torino, whose goal was a Giorgio Bresciani penalty. We were out of the Coppa Italia while Verona went through. I told you that place brought me bad luck.

I sounded the alarm. I asked the club to approach UEFA and request the second leg of the Vitosha match be moved at least a couple of days from October 6 to 8, so that I could get a few players back. I also used the press to flash a warning sign to the Milanello dressing rooms: "We scored two goals in Sofia, but we can easily lose three at home," I said.

I deliberately left out one detail. Among the returning players, even though he had still to reach 100 per cent, was a centre-forward called Marco van Basten.

CHAMPAGNE! AND VAN BASTEN'S PAYING!

European Cup
First round, second leg
Milan 5 Vitosha Sofia 2

Van Basten had a very particular character. He was meteoropathic, he could literally change with the weather – a difference in air pressure or temperature seemed to provoke an injury. But he was also a brilliant player whom I wouldn't have swapped even for the best striker of the modern era – the Brazilian Ronaldo.

He was a good guy and an exceptional champion whose talent was truly unique. In the beginning, I worked hard to make him understand that we Italians were not primitive beasts. If he had a callus on his foot, he went to a Dutch podiatrist. If he had toothache, he went to a Dutch dentist. If he needed a haircut, he went to a Dutch barber.

I used to say to him: "Just remember, Marco, that when we were winning World Cups, you were still under water."

In the end, we convinced him, not least because it was at Milan that he became Van Basten. He never won the

Ballon d'Or in Holland. One time when he came back from national team duty, Marco said to me: "Boss, Milan play better than Holland and I have more fun here."

On another occasion, we were watching a Pescara v Napoli game on TV together at Milanello. Giovanni Galeone's Pescara laid siege to Napoli, who just couldn't manage to get out or connect with their strikers. I said, "Marco, would you have liked to play in Maradona's Napoli?"

His response? "If that's the way they play, I'd soon be leaving."

It took time and quite a few cases of champagne to win his trust and overcome his very Dutch snobbery, but in the end he became one of the most convinced champions of the cause, because he understood that our game made him great.

Someone like Rijkaard would have done well in another Italian club – they would have taken the same advantage of his athletic strength. But Van Basten could not have found another team built to always attack, to stay tight and compact around him, ready to service him continually.

Champagne? We bet a case each time.

I would needle him: "Marco, I'll set out four defenders, you put together a team of 10 – you'll not be needing a goalkeeper. We get to clear the ball beyond half-way, then you go and retrieve it. If you manage to score once in 15 minutes, your team wins."

I wanted to show him that four well-organised players are stronger than 10 who improvise. His team attacked and attacked but they never scored. If I had made Van Basten hand over all the cases of champagne I won from him, I'd still be drinking now.

I challenged him to an arm wrestle, too. Neither of us

managed to get the other man's arm down. He began to suspect that I hadn't been fully trying, and indeed he was right. I had really strong, well-trained arms. I could chest press 90 kilos. Once I challenged Edgar Davids to see who could manage more reps with the bar using a single arm: it finished 10-apiece.

To show Marco the right position to take up when pressing, I had to shout into the megaphone a thousand times. Another thousand times, I had to draw him a diagram. I had to make him understand that, when our attack was over, he shouldn't just take a rest up a siding – he needed to stay in an active position, ready to receive a pass or to hunt down the ball. When the lesson entered his brain and he was fully convinced of his own worth, Marco became a phenomenon at pressing, too.

Everyone remembers Baresi's forward runs, him leading forth the defensive line with his arms spread wide like an aeroplane. Or Gullit furiously chasing down the ball with his dreadlocks billowing in the wind. Few recall the spite with which Marco hunted an opponent when he pressed. Awareness, that little burst and then – bang! – he was on top of him. Van Basten was a piranha.

Not long ago, out for dinner with Rijkaard, Marco confessed: "Frank, we should put up a statue to Sacchi for teaching us pressing."

As a coach, he learned the lesson even more fully and was able to see differently the misunderstandings that had often caused us to argue in the early days.

When I left Milan, I gave the team a talk. Despite what some have written, it's not true that I said: "Without me, you'll not win anything anymore." I said something quite different. "You can still win trophies, but not in the same way. Not with our style."

Trophies aren't the only thing that makes a team. It's also about its recognisability, its way of being unique – its style.

I then said something else. "With everything you've learned, you're football professors now. You can all become good coaches."

From that side, three national team managers (Donadoni, Rijkaard, Van Basten) have emerged, as well as two Champions League winning coaches (Ancelotti and Rijkaard). Knowledge isn't enough to become a good coach, however. You also need passion and professionalism. Gullit, for example, did not have passion. Naturally, I'm very fond of Ancelotti, who started coaching at my side, but I have to say that it's in Van Basten's teams that I've seen my football, done well.

One time, when he was coaching Holland, he confessed to me: "Boss, now that I've gone over to the other side, I can see how many problems I caused you."

I replied: "Marco, if it's any consolation, you should know that you solved plenty for me too."

For example, on the evening of October 6, 1988, against Vitosha Sofia, in a game we approached with a few worries because of the many absentees. After a quarter of an hour, Van Basten had already scored twice: the first a left-footed strike after a Virdis header set him up, the second via a Donadoni assist after the midfielder won the ball back with a brilliant press in the Bulgarians' half. Pressing is the key to everything.

The third goal came from a bit of goalmouth robbery and the fourth was scored by Marco a few minutes from the end. A great swan-dive of a header. Just to complete the set, Van Basten had also delivered the assist for Virdis' goal. It finished 5-2. Riding the crest of a wave, Marco announced excitedly to the media: "I want Gullit's Ballon d'Or." With the excellent European Championships he'd just had, he was already a good way down the line. Donadoni had a great game, too.

In the San Siro that night, there were more than 50,000 people for a tie that, regardless of my worries, had already been won in the first leg. By now, people were coming to the stadium for the pure pleasure of watching us play, just as you would go to the theatre. That knowledge gave me even more satisfaction than qualifying for the next round.

In my grey diary, I wrote:

> *Excellent game, well played, with lots of passes and movement without the ball. We conceded twice because we slackened off. At times, the team isn't as compact as it should be.*

Looking ahead to the draw with the media, president Berlusconi said he hoped we didn't get Real Madrid. "It's too early for that," he explained. "They're the most worthy rival for us to play in a great final. Any other team would suit us just fine."

We drew Red Star Belgrade, a team rich in talent and in pride, who would win the European Cup a couple of years later. They would be a tough opponent, especially in the imposing, red-hot Marakana. In the first round, the Yugoslavs had had great fun beating Dundalk 8-0 on aggregate.

Before we thought about them, however, we had to concentrate on the league, which was finally kicking off after the South Korean Olympics. We wore the scudetto on our breasts.

Our first game was against Fiorentina at the San Siro on October 19 and we won well, 4-0. Virdis scored a hat-trick and the other goal came from Donadoni. This time, Van Basten didn't score, and he blamed his father for it: "When Joop comes to the stadium to watch me, I never find the back of the net."

Not everything was as straightforward as the scoreline suggests. In my log-book I wrote:

> *Important win, even if the team played without much clarity, speed or intensity. Their legs and heads all looked foggy. A few bits of individual brilliance made the difference.*

That doesn't sound like we won 4-0. But, as I've said before in these pages, when the team had managed a good result, and was more receptive and creative as a consequence, that's when I went hard with my criticisms to show where and how they could improve.

My sense was that, despite the big win, the team had problems. They had looked tired and blurry and, after beating Pescara away 3-1, we produced a bad performance at home to Lazio in what should have been the dress rehearsal for Red Star. Gullit, making his first league appearance of the season, hobbled about for an hour before I took him off.

Speaking to the media post-match, he admitted: "I'm only 10% fit right now." He said he would miss the game three days later, or at the very least he wouldn't start. My concern is writ large in the log book:

> *Good result, for how we played. A lesser team could have lost. We're paying the price for a big drop-off, caused, perhaps, by the thought that it's possible to achieve a lot giving little. This drop-off is not allowing*

MAGGIO

ore 10,30
10' STRETCH + GG.
15' SCHEMI OFF 11:0
5' TORELLO 5:2 10x10 1 TOCCO
5' TIRI SCARICO STOP 30''
* RIGORI

STEAU BUCAREST - MILAN 0/4
GULLIT 2
VAN BAST. 2

24 Mercoledì

FANTASTICI!!!

GALLI
TASSOTTI COSTACURTA (75' GALLI) BARESI MALDINI
COLOMBO RIJKAARD ANCELOTTI
DONADONI
GULLIT (60' VIRDIS) VAN BASTEN
PINATO NUCIARI - EVANI

Sacchi's 1988/89 diary – in which he kept his writing "really small so as to fit in as much information and as many reflections as possible" – reached its climax on May 24, 1989, when his Milan side destroyed Steaua Bucharest 4-0 in the Camp Nou to lift the European Cup. "When I get back to the hotel, I pick up my log-book and for the first time since I started compiling it, I write a single word. Just one. Fantastic!"

Settimana di lavoro pre-raduno
(3 sedute settimanali) utile soprattutto per
le ultime 2 settimane pre-raduno.

1) 10' Stretching
15' Corsa continua
4 volte balzi quintupli alternati Dx e Sn
4 " " DECUPLI " " " "
10' Addominali
10 x 100mt in leggera progressione + PARTE LATERALE DEL CAMPO IN SOUPLESSE. (VELOCITÀ 50-70%)

2) Stretching
6 volte 20 mt. skip (corsa ginocchia ben alte)
3 volte 50 mt (½ campo calcio) a balzi alternati.
20' corsa a ritmo alterno (2' lenti + 1' a ritmo superiore)

3) 10' Stretching
10' Lavori x muscolatura addominale
6 x 10 richiami ginocchia al petto.
10 x 100mt in leggera progressione (velocità 50-70%)
15' corsa continua a ritmo leggermente crescente.

N.B. OGNI SEDUTA DEVE ESSERE COMPLETATA DA 15' A 30' DI TECNICA (ESERCIZI VARI) SPECIALMENTE

Sacchi obsessively documented every detail of his time with Milan, including training drills, reflections on matches and observations about individual players. The 'Smemoranda' diary – as well as providing the backbone for this book – also gave him material for uncompromising teamtalks. "In front of the team, I would read out even the harshest comments. In fact, *especially* the harshest comments, to give them a shake and provoke a reaction."

Sacchi's groundbreaking style was built on training-ground toil. His obsession with intensive pressing required endless repetition and extremely high levels of fitness. Sacchi would push his players to greater extremes by shouting instructions through a megaphone. "'I hear Arrigo doesn't shout anymore, he's got himself a megaphone,' my wife said to Tassotti one day. 'That's not strictly true,' said Tasso. 'Now he shouts into the megaphone.'" *Imago*

The Milanello training centre was the base for Sacchi's revolution. When he took over in 1987, he wrote the players a letter outlining his expectations. It also included a training programme that they would have to undertake ahead of their pre-season camp. "I believe that when the players received the letter, most of them suspected they had ended up in the hands of a madman." *Imago*

The relationship between Sacchi and Milan chairman Silvio Berlusconi was the foundation for the club's domestic and European success. The pair first became acquainted in 1986, when Sacchi's Parma – newly promoted to Serie B – twice beat Milan in the space of seven months. On his first meeting with Berlusconi, Sacchi said: "After only a few words, I had the strong, clear feeling that I'd known that man my whole life. I realised right from that first moment that we were cut from the same cloth; that we were both born to dream big." *Imago*

Prior to Sacchi's appointment at Milan, chairman Silvio Berlusconi had been seduced by the talents of Argentinos Juniors striker Claudio Borghi, above. He signed him in 1986 with a view to Borghi starting his Serie A career in 1988/89, the season that UEFA's new 'three foreigner' rule came into force. However, Sacchi was not convinced of Borghi's character and insisted on the signing of Frank Rijkaard from Sporting Lisbon. Sacchi said: "Mr President… if we go with Borghi, we lose everything. Me, you and Milan. If you've chosen to keep him, I can't stay." Sacchi's ultimatum paid off and Milan signed Rijkaard, below, the last member of their Dutch trio *Imago*

Angelo Colombo – shooting in the 1-0 win over Werder Bremen in the 1989 European Cup quarter-final first leg, above – was a journeyman who had just been relegated with Udinese when Sacchi brought him to the San Siro. His intelligent running at both ends of the pitch set the tempo for the team's pressing game during a memorable three-year spell. Chairman Silvio Berlusconi once said to Sacchi: "I haven't spent 100 billion [Lire] to watch Colombo play!" to which Sacchi replied, "As long as I'm manager, whoever deserves to play, will play." *Imago*

Pietro Paolo Virdis, below, was entering the veteran years of his career when Sacchi arrived at Milan, but his ruthless finishing made him an important asset as back-up striker to Ruud Gullit and Marco van Basten. In the 1988/89 European Cup run, he scored three times in the first three matches, against Vitosha Sofia and Red Star Belgrade. "He was great at always being ready, and at making the most of his opportunities," said Sacchi *Imago*

Franco Baresi was one of the initial sceptics when confronted with Sacchi's attacking approach. However, he soon flourished in the sweeper role and became a convert. Sacchi said: "One week, I reduced the training load because I thought the team looked tired. Franco Baresi came to tell me: 'Boss, if we don't work on our defensive movements, we risk them no longer being second nature.' Him, one of the most sceptical of all to begin with." *Imago*

The success of Sacchi's Milan remains synonymous with the abundant gifts of their three Dutchmen (left to right) Frank Rijkaard, Marco van Basten and Ruud Gullit. The latter two scored 13 goals between them en route to winning the European Cup in 1989, and both netted twice in the 4-0 victory over Steaua Bucharest in the final *Imago*

Sacchi and Van Basten had a volatile relationship, but the Dutchman adapted his game to accommodate Sacchi's style. "Everyone remembers Baresi's forward runs, him leading forth the defensive line with his arms spread wide like an aeroplane," Sacchi said. "Or Gullit furiously chasing down the ball with his dreadlocks billowing in the wind. Few recall the spite with which Marco hunted an opponent when he pressed. Awareness, that little burst and then – bang! – he was on top of him. Van Basten was a piranha." *Imago*

Milan's trip to Yugoslavia to face Red Star Belgrade in the second leg of their European Cup second round tie in November 1988 turned into one of the most extraordinary episodes in the history of European football. A dense fog descended on the Marakana during the match, causing Sacchi to miss both Dejan Savicevic's opening goal for Red Star and the sending off of Virdis. The match was abandoned after 57 minutes and rescheduled for the following day, with Milan eventually winning 4-1 on penalties *Alamy*

The team photo from before kick-off in the 1989 European Cup final at the Camp Nou. Back row left to right: Paolo Maldini, Marco van Basten, Ruud Gullit, Carlo Ancelotti, Frank Rijkaard, Giovanni Galli; Front row left to right: Franco Baresi, Roberto Donadoni, Alessandro Costacurta, Angelo Colombo, Mauro Tassotti *Imago*

Marco van Basten and Ruud Gullit both scored twice in the 1989 European Cup final. Gullit's opening goal, above, arrived after 18 minutes and, as Sacchi stated: "The roar of the crowd makes the Barcelona sky shake." Van Basten added another with a thumping header, below, less than 10 minutes later, in what would become one of the most one-sided European finals of all time *Getty / Imago*

Left to right: Roberto Donadoni, Ruud Gullit, Paolo Maldini and Angelo Colombo celebrate after the final whistle in the 1989 European Cup final. Victory was a poignant moment for Donadoni in particular, who almost died on the pitch during Milan's second round, second leg replay v Red Star Belgrade. The Italian was given mouth-to-mouth after being knocked out by an elbow to the face. He went on to make a full recovery and end the season with a European Cup winners' medal *Getty*

Carlo Ancelotti – raising the 1989 European Cup trophy aloft – was one of Sacchi's most inspired signings. The midfielder had endured three meniscus and two cruciate ligament operations before his move from Roma to Milan. Chairman Silvio Berlusconi expressed his doubts about Ancelotti, but Sacchi told him. "I need a brain in the middle of the pitch… If you sign him for me, I'll win the league. Definitely." *Getty*

Sacchi arrived at Milan with the intention of playing Paolo Maldini at right-back, to take advantage of his stronger right foot, but changed his mind after one practice session. Maldini would go on to make the left-back slot his own and become a defensive colossus for the Rossoneri
Getty

Sacchi fell in love with the European Cup when watching footage of the great Real Madrid team of the 1950s. The lifelong love affair with the tournament was consummated on the evening of May 24, 1989, when he finally got his hands on the famous trophy
Getty

us to play our game and show our quality. Sub-consciously, many players are already thinking about the European Cup.

There is precariousness in all success. If you win but aren't used to winning, there are two big risks: you can feel invincible or you can feel sated. People who aren't used to success struggle to find the right balance. We shouldn't forget that, in that Milan team, there were young men who had been at the club for eight or nine years and won very little. I'd also won very little, but for me, these were all new, exciting things. Having just come from Serie C and B, there's no way I could be lacking motivation.

Playing for the first time in a prestigious competition like the European Cup definitely took something away from us in the league. The troubled, worrisome build-up to the first game against Red Star finished in the worst possible way when Chicco Evani – such a big part of our tactical balance – suffered an injury on the eve of battle.

Unfortunately, all these negative omens presaged a difficult match.

THE BOOK OF VIRDIS

European Cup
Second round, first leg
Milan 1 Red Star Belgrade 1

I knew two things in particular about the Yugoslavs' game: that they were spiteful and that they were technical. Spiteful to the point of unfairness, and powered by ferocious motivations. They still led modest lives over there and looked at our country like Napoleon's hungry soldiers before the Italian campaign. The only way to enjoy our riches was to beat us.

Yugoslavian football has often had great champions but rarely great teams, because they've never managed to transform the abundant individual talent into collective strength.

Robert Prosinecki and Dejan Savicevic, for example, both had a lot of class, but they kept it to themselves. When they played together, you really needed two balls, one for each of them. Dragon Stojkovic, by contrast, was a more complete champion, a true player. In the three games that we played against Red Star, he caused us plenty of difficulty. He would later spend a season (1991/92) with Verona, and in 1993 he was part of the Marseille team that beat Milan in the first Champions League final.

Savicevic would score and contribute an assist for Stojkovic in Belgrade, but as far as attitude is concerned, he was closer to Borghi than my ideal prototype. Sadly, I would later coach him at Milan when I returned in 1996.

There were more than 70,000 people in the San Siro for that first leg, all dressed up for a party. It was our first serious outing in the European Cup. I played Tassotti and Mussi at full-back, with Paolo Maldini and Baresi in the middle. The midfield four were Colombo, Rijkaard, Ancelotti and Donadoni, with Virdis and Van Basten up front. Gullit was on the bench.

It was a hard, agonising match. As the league games had shown us, we were not in top form.

Red Star surprised us at the start of the second half. Stojkovic set off on the counter-attack with the ball at his feet. He evaded Baresi before hitting a shot with the outside of his boot that was pretty central, but which Giovanni Galli couldn't manage to save. Our response was immediate. Barely a minute later, we equalised when Virdis ran on to a lovely through ball from Van Basten and produced a brilliantly cool finish.

Pietro Paolo Virdis scored lots of important goals for us, like his double at the San Paolo in the game where we beat Napoli to go above them in the race for the scudetto. He had all the qualities you look for in a pedigree striker, from his shooting technique to the ruthlessness of his finishing. He didn't have everything I wanted in my ideal attacker, but when I arrived at Milan I kept him in the squad, partly because he'd been top-scorer the previous season. You never get rid of people who score more goals than everyone else.

I asked him for new things, and he forced himself to do them with professionalism and dedication. He was already in his thirties – a time when players usually believe they have nothing left to learn. One day, after he scored a goal in the derby by stealing the ball from Daniel Passarella, Italo Alllodi – who had brought me to Fiorentina – called me and said: "Arrigo, if you've managed to convince Virdis to press, you can do anything in this world. Every time I see it, I still can't believe it."

I believe I extended Pietro Paolo's breadth of knowledge, and I also reckon I prolonged his career with our training methods. But the reverse is also true: he expanded my own knowledge into different areas. He taught me not to be prejudiced towards players whose characteristics seemed distant from my style of football, and to ask them for things that they could actually give. Big players make possible what coaches believe improbable. And vice versa.

When Gullit and Van Basten were fully fit, Virdis dropped out of the starting line-up. He was an intelligent man and accepted the hierarchy quite calmly. And anyway, the injury to Van Basten in the first season and Gullit's bumps and bruises in the second meant he was still a major figure in the first couple of years of my Milan. He was great at always being ready, and at making the most of his opportunities. At the end of the season – at the age of 32 – he moved to Lecce to spend the last part of his career there.

Pietro Paolo was a cultured man of few words. On the bus en-route to games, he would read, even if I sometimes suspected it was always the same book.

Unfortunately, after netting his goal that night, Virdis missed another great chance where it seemed easier to score. Donadoni hit the crossbar and Stevan Stojanovic made a miraculous save.

Due to a combination of bad luck and the shameful playacting of the visitors, who wasted time wherever they could, the game stayed locked at 1-1. Not even Gullit, who came on in imperfect condition in the second half, could manage to shift the dial.

In his post-match comments, Berlusconi attacked Red Star's filibuster tactic of feigning injury to break up the game and deny us rhythm. He condemned the Yugoslavian stuntmen and promised with that unshakeable optimism of his: "We'll win in Belgrade!"

It was more an order than a prediction.

Speaking to the media, I underlined: "We missed Evani terribly."

Unlike Virdis, Chicco was born for my kind of football. He had the feet, the technique and the brain to really succeed in it. He was a unique midfielder who gave our 4-4-2 real balance, and our game elevated Chicco at the same time. It made sense of his qualities, it increased his self-belief and, as a consequence, it gave him the one thing he lacked: personality.

The best system is one which allows you immediate and natural responses, if these have been internalised. Certainty comes from this and the knowledge that you're always connected to a team who will transmit to you their strength.

At the start, when we played Napoli and Chicco went up against Fernando De Napoli, who had a quicker burst of pace on the flank, he was always worried. I told him: "Don't worry. You'll always have two or three teammates close at hand, ready to protect you. At best, De Napoli will have Alessandro Renica running in from 40m away."

In seven years, Evani had only scored two goals, both of them against Catania. I would say to him: "Catania must reckon you've got it in for them. If you move together with the team, you'll score at least five goals every season."

That night, the crowd filtered out of the San Siro disappointed. The draw already put at risk our involvement in the European Cup. Red Star only needed a 0-0 to knock us out, and given how they'd behaved in Milan, we could already imagine how they would go about achieving that draw in Belgrade's Marakana.

The players were also dejected. The day after the game, the meteoropathic Van Basten had a head full of dark clouds. In the dressing room, in front of everyone, he said: "We're already out."

I decided to give everyone a shake. I invented a phone call from Berlusconi and told the boys, "the president has just instructed me to tell you that he didn't spend 100 billion [Lire] for us to go out in the second round of the European Cup!"

It was the right moment to encourage hope and optimism.

In my log-book I made the following comments about the 1-1 draw:

> *Great effort and desire, but that wasn't enough. In a game, you reap what you've sown in the preceding weeks. The many incidents we've experienced go beyond bad luck to a lack of attention, endurance and motivation. We've been punished by the result and our performance, but I'm not worried. If this team, in all its constituent parts, can rediscover motivation, enthusiasm and will, we'll win in Belgrade. Even a 1-0 win at home would have been harsh on us. But luck has to be earned and perhaps we didn't do everything we could have to deserve it. Mentally, we*

were further on than was the case against Lazio. Give me humility and will once more and we'll soon be smiling again.

I managed to indirectly transmit another message of serenity to the team. Instead of holing myself up inside Milanello and stewing in front of the tactics board thinking about the Marakana, I was a guest on the *Game of Nines,* a Channel 5 quiz show hosted by Raimondo Vianello and Sandra Mondaini. I was struck by Raimondo's great professionalism. While all the guests were laughing and joking in the minutes before the show began, he went over and over the schedule with ferocious concentration. The same thing we would require at the Marakana.

The performance against Juventus in Turin on October 30 – our fourth league game – gave us good grounds for optimism. It finished 0-0 but we dominated from start to finish and kept the *bianconeri* hemmed in. They were totally unable to react. I started all three Dutch players and I'd got Evani back as well.

In the pages of that grey Smemoranda, my satisfaction is clear:

Good result – we've gone back to being a team. Everyone playing our game with and for their teammates. A big step forward. We rediscovered the right mental state. Now we'll rediscover the right physical and technical ones. Our enemies are arrogance, egotism and childishness. It was easy to see the big difference in our play and our ability to stay organised on the pitch. We showed imagination and knowledge. They didn't enjoy themselves, but we did. Hard work pays off and so does respect for the game and for your teammates. Think, don't vegetate: football starts in the head, not the feet.

We started well the following Sunday against Verona, too. Strangely, Van Basten missed a couple of easy chances, but we went ahead in the 23rd minute thanks to a lovely right-footed strike from Gullit, whose condition was improving with each game.

It was an important match, the dress rehearsal for Belgrade. I sent out the team that would start at the Marakana, with Rijkaard playing in central defence alongside Franco Baresi. Ten minutes after his goal, however, Gullit hit a long ball for Colombo, felt something in his left thigh and asked to come off. Injured again! A nightmare start to the season. It looked like a strain. The initial feeling was that we would be without him for at least 10 days, and that he definitely wouldn't play against Red Star. Gullit himself seemed to have given in at full-time: "It's a shame. I would really have liked to play in Belgrade. I must have done too much training in this cold."

Some people suspected we had rushed him back, but in truth his re-introduction had been gradual. Half an hour against Red Star, 70 minutes against Juventus and then half an hour in Verona before he pulled up.

By contrast, Virdis felt like he was already at the Marakana. "I'm sorry for Ruud, but I'll happily play. Here at Milan, unfortunately, it's a real battle to win your place."

With great honesty, Pietro Paolo admitted that for the strike which put us 2-1 up, Roberto Solda's deflection on Van Basten's shot had been crucial, and as such it was an own goal. Marco, from the great height of his Dutch pride, corrected him: "What own goal are you talking about? The ball swerved because of a special effect – the Van

Basten effect."

We would be entering the formidable arena of the Marakana without our lion, without our Ballon d'Or winner who had rediscovered the way to goal, without Ruud Gullit. But the Red Devils had shown in Verona that we were ready for the hell of Belgrade. Above all, in a year and a half of work, everyone had learned that our true strength was our game, not this or that individual player.

And it would be our game which roared in that arena.

A TIGER IN THE FOG

European Cup
Second round, second leg
Red Star Belgrade 1 Milan 0
(match abandoned due to fog after 57 minutes)

Hell began long before the game itself, in our morning run-through. We heard repeated explosions from outside the stadium, but nobody paid any notice. The players probably thought it was firecrackers or bangers. Being someone who occasionally went to the shooting gallery in Milan, I realised straight away that those were bursts of machine gun fire.

It was Commander Arkan's Tigers, a Serbian paramilitary organisation which, during the war in the ex-Yugoslavia, committed the most awful crimes in the name of ethnic cleansing. The little army belonging to Zeljko Raznatovic, Commander Arkan, who was later assassinated, was made up for the most part of Red Star Ultras and former prisoners.

Years later, I went back to Belgrade with Atletico Madrid to play FK Obilic, the club where Arkan was president. The day before the game, we trained in Obilic's little stadium. We heard a strange noise, a kind of roaring that came from behind the dressing rooms. We went to have a look. It was a real roar, not a *kind of* roar: there was a tiger in a cage. On the evening of the game, which was played in Partizan's stadium, Arkan walked across the pitch before kick-off with the tiger on a leash. At the finish, Arkan reached me as I was heading down the staircase which led to the dressing rooms. He touched my shoulder and said: "Mr Sacchi, once again you've been damn lucky in Belgrade."

It was true: we'd won without deserving to. The "once again" was a reference to the fog.

On the evening of Wednesday November 9, 1988, the Marakana was jam-packed – 100,000 super-charged souls. I sent out the same starting team I had in Verona, with the exception of Virdis, who replaced Gullit. We'd tried everything we could to get Ruud on the pitch, invoking a secret strategy that criss-crossed the skies of Europe.

At 8pm the night before the game, he underwent a fitness test on the eighth floor of the Hotel Continental: little runs along the corridor. It didn't tell us much either way. He returned to his room and made a call back to Holland, to Ted Troost, who was a friend and confessor as well as his trusted physio. He told Troost how he was feeling then came back to see us. Ruud advised: "Go and get him."

At 6am the following morning, a small plane took off from Berne. It picked up Troost in Amsterdam, moved on to Rome to collect Galliani, then headed to Belgrade. At 9am, Ruud did a second test in the gardens of the hotel. It wasn't very encouraging. "There's something not right," he said.

At 11am, the Dutch physio arrived at the Continental and spoke at length with Gullit, treated him, then went to consult our own doctors. Before getting on the bus to the Marakana, Ruud did a third and final test that gave us a bit more hope. Ted Troost gave him a massage and decided: "He can play one half. Any more would be risky."

I put him on the bench.

From the kick-off, instead of playing the ball, Red Star gave it to us, as if to say: "On you come – we'll be laughing."

It was a provocation designed to show us that they would be holing themselves up in defence, and that they would use any means necessary to obtain the 0-0 draw to send them through to the quarter-finals. I'd only seen tactics like this once before, from Varese when I was coaching Parma. They would deliberately go offside to interrupt our moves.

We kept impotently bouncing off the Red Star blockade. We attacked, but without the necessary pace and determination. And then everything disappeared in the fog. A fog so thick that you could have driven a nail into it. A milky dough, dense, impenetrable, coloured yellow by the stadium floodlights.

Five minutes after half-time, someone appeared out of nowhere, came over to the bench and told us that Savicevic had put Red Star 1-0 up. We hadn't even realised. It was absurd to keep playing in those conditions.

I got up and moved towards the pitch to protest, but there was no point because the referee, immersed in that yellow-grey hank, had no chance of seeing me. Fortunately, seven minutes later German official Dieter Pauly decided of his own accord to suspend the match. In the dressing room, I found myself facing Virdis, who already had his civvies on.

"What's going on here?" I asked, dumbfounded.

"I was sent off," replied Pietro Paolo. We'd missed that

too. It meant that, when the game was suspended, we were a goal down, a man down and with only half an hour to pull it back. Practically out. But I hadn't known – the fog had kept fear hidden from us as well.

Regardless, I'd like to remind people that in my career, I've won plenty games with 10 men. Even with Italy.

I asked Galliani to fine Virdis for his sending off and also Ancelotti for the booking that would keep him out of the rematch the following day. Kick-off was set for 1pm, and we'd start again at 0-0.

I spent a large part of the night going between the players' rooms. I told them all: "We're that bloke who trips and falls onto the tracks, but the train rumbles past without even touching him. We're talking about the strength of the survivor who knows he has good fortune on his side. That's what we are. Tomorrow we'll show that strength on the field."

After that, I told them what I thought were the necessary ingredients for success: "Eyes, memory, patience and *bus de cul*."

"Eyes" meant attitude, "memory" meant learning, "patience" meant patience and "*bus de cul*" good luck. We already had the last one – now all we had to do was put in place the other three.

As I went back into my room, knowing I would struggle to sleep, I saw Rijkaard walking up and down the corridor, counting with his fingers and repeating to himself: "Eyes, memory, patience and *bus de cul*." It sounded like he was reciting the rosary.

Gullit, meanwhile, made light of it. "Berlusconi was born with a silver spoon in his mouth. I reckon he caused the fog himself with his cigars."

A long night delivered us to judgement day. I needed

that time to think about the team I would send out, even if I didn't really have many options.

Virdis and Ancelotti were missing and I could only turn to Gullit for a maximum of one half, and only in an emergency. I no longer had Daniele Massaro, who had gone out on loan to Roma in September. It was me who asked for him to be sold. He hadn't conducted himself well during our European pre-season friendlies. He either warmed up poorly or came on without the right motivation. And he always had some little problem – I don't know whether he was a hypochondriac or if he needed to be the centre of attention. At Fiorentina, they'd called him Lazarus, because he was always struggling during the week, came back to life on the Saturday then played on the Sunday. Once, before a friendly, he lay down on the massage table, with an ice pack on each knee and a third on his ankle. Gullit walked past, took one of the packs and put it on his head: "That's where you need cooled down."

In my first year, the day before an important game, some of the players were listening to the Milan psychologist talk about concentration techniques. We suddenly heard shots. It was Massaro concentrating in his own way: he'd set up a target in the Milanello woods and was practising his shooting. Naturally, I didn't play him in the game: "You've already played enough."

After a short time, Daniele called me from Rome, begging me to let him come back. "I'll be the first to arrive for training and the last to leave. You'll never have reason to moan about me again," he said.

Because I'm someone who likes to have faith in people, I brought him back to Milan. Massaro kept his promise. As Italy manager, I called him up to the national team and played him in the 1994 World Cup final.

When people assess our achievement in that 1988/89 European Cup, they always overlook one key factor: our squad. I had 19 players, three of whom were goalkeepers. Our reserves were Mussi, Bianchi, Mannari, Cappellini – all kids. Looking back, it seems impossible that Milan managed to do what we did with the squad reduced to the bare bones, active on three fronts, continually challenged by injuries and faced with my training sessions, which, as the log book attests, were so demanding.

To remember only the Milan of the three Dutchmen, the Milan of Baresi and Maldini, is to do a great disservice to the group who – despite the reduced resources available – pulled off an immense, absolutely unrepeatable success.

A comparison with today's squads tells the full story of that masterpiece. Let's consider the Juventus season 2018/19 roll call, for example. On their bench, you could find a complete second team of fully formed players.

On November 10, 1988, in the inferno of the Marakana in a match that our whole season was riding on, I started Graziano Mannari, a 19-year-old lad. The Yugoslavian TV folks didn't even know how to spell his name, and so in the pre-match team graphic it appeared as: "11 Grazzianno."

In extra time, the key, most delicate moment of the match, I replaced him with Massimiliano Cappellini who was 17 and whom I'd then ask to take one of the five penalties in the shoot-out.

There was an incredible tension on the bus that took us to the stadium. Nobody breathed. We went into the dressing room at the Marakana, which was already roaring with passion, and it was then that Adriano Galliani made one of the very few errors of his splendid career.

BOSS, THE KID IS SHAKING

European Cup
Second round, second leg replay
Red Star Belgrade 1 Milan 1
(after extra time, Milan win 4-1 on penalties)

Galliani walked into the dressing room and announced: "There must be at least 120,000 fans out there. They've opened the gates, and where before there was a single row of people, there are three now. But you mustn't be afraid."

Him saying, "You mustn't be afraid" really meant "You should be".

It was just as well that Gullit, our team's courage, intervened by asking: "How many people normally turn out here?"

"40-50,000," replied Galliani.

"Good," concluded Gullit. "That means all the rest have come to see us."

Milan went out onto the field with the heart of a lion. We were much more determined, reactive and sparkling than the previous day and we went after Red Star from the off. The fog had disappeared; the sun was shining but it was still a freezing cold day. After four minutes, we took the lead. Evani shot from outside the area, defender Goran Vasilijevic tried to clear on the volley but sliced it and the ball span backwards. Vasilijevic managed to reach it, but by the time he booted it clear, it had already gone over the line. It wasn't a question of inches, but of feet. They used the still image to measure the distance, and it was 110cm. Only the German referee, Dieter Pauly, didn't see, or didn't want to see. He waved play on.

It was totally absurd. At the moment he struck the ball, Vasilijevic's back was touching the net. As Bruno Pizzul said during Rai's live TV broadcast: "It was a very obvious, self-evident goal."

Despite this gross injustice, we got our heads down and continued to attack, with good movement and team play. Tassotti and Maldini were constantly pushing hard, and in the 34th minute the goal we deserved arrived. We won a free-kick in their defensive third, to the left of centre. Evani touched the ball to Donadoni, who looked up and measured a perfect parabola to take it to the far post. Van Basten jumped higher than everyone and bulleted a header into the net.

At that point, we were through. For the first time in the tie, Red Star found themselves needing to attack and not just defend, as they had at the San Siro and up to now in the Marakana. Unfortunately, it only took them four minutes to draw level. We allowed ourselves to be taken by surprise.

Goran Juric hit a long free-kick out of defence, Savicevic controlled it with his chest in midfield, turned and played the ball deep for Stojkovic. Their captain let the ball bounce then blasted an unstoppable shot under the crossbar: 1-1. Everything perfectly balanced.

Shortly afterwards, in the 43rd minute, Vasilijevic – the

bloke who scored the own goal that wasn't seen – went in violently on Donadoni, hitting him with a headbutt and an elbow at the same time. Roberto hit the deck, knocked out. These were minutes of true terror: he looked dead. Players were waving their arms about and putting their hands on their heads. Even the Red Star guys. They had immediately understood the seriousness of the situation. A few players had to move away, shocked, from the scene.

Angelo Pagani, our masseur, was the first to reach Donadoni. He managed to open his mouth, which was jammed shut because of his fractured jaw. His tongue had gone right back, which threatened to suffocate him. Dr Monti gave him mouth-to-mouth. Roberto showed no sign of life, and then he began to stamp his feet on the ground, which often happens to people who have suffered cranial trauma.

Maldini told us later: "He was blue, with his eyes wide open, and he was stamping his feet like an animal in the slaughterhouse."

The most affected teammate of all was Van Basten, who ran to us on the bench shouting, "A doctor! A doctor!" He then hugged Paolo Taveggia, our general manager, and burst out crying like a child. He didn't want to play anymore. We managed to calm him down and convince him to carry on, as Roberto was carried off on a stretcher.

At half-time, an announcement was made over the public address system at the Marakana. It was roundly booed by the whole crowd. When they translated it into Italian, we understood why. The announcer had wanted to reassure fans who had seen Donadoni lie on the turf for so long without moving, by telling them the good news coming from the hospital. Roberto had regained consciousness and, apart from that fractured jaw, no serious damage appeared to have been done. There were no brain lesions.

Arkan's pals and all the other Red Star fans were booing Roberto's good health. This infuriated Gullit and the other players, who went back onto the field even more ferocious and fired-up. We were now the tigers. They'd chalked off a perfectly good goal and put one of our players in hospital, then booed the news of his recovery.

I went looking for the referee, grabbed him by the collar and called him a cheat to his face. He must have had a guilty conscience, because he didn't make mention of this in his report. Years later, when I was a Parma director, I met Pauly in Moscow and went to say hello. He was there as a referee liaison officer for the match.

"Do you remember?" I asked in English, looking him straight in the eye. "I remember," he replied, lowering his gaze.

The second half and extra time were played against a backdrop of deafening bedlam. If the Marakana ever truly looked and sounded like hell, it was that day. We kept attacking, creating more than them, but we couldn't score. We were exhausted.

Gullit, who had come on for Donadoni and was only supposed to play one half, ended up playing the last part of the first half, then the whole of the second half and extra time. He was wearing cycling shorts under his match ones to keep his muscles warm on that bitterly cold afternoon. I feared that from one moment to the next he would pull up, touching his leg with a pained grimace on his face. At that point, who knows how long we'd have lost him for? I even asked him if he wanted to come off during extra time. He replied: "I'm going nowhere. It's time to fight. If I don't push it a bit in a game like this, when do I?"

Ruud was our courage, our general in battle. The Milan

shirt had got under his skin, just as it had with Franco Baresi, our captain, who gave a monumental performance, managing to transmit calm and strength to everyone else in that hell-hole. Every time he came out with the ball at his feet, the flames of hell made way.

Pauly blew for the end of extra time. Our future in the European Cup now depended on five penalty kicks.

I wanted Van Basten to take the first, but Marco preferred to take the second. At this point, Baresi stepped forward and said: "I'm taking the first one."

I assigned the third to Evani, the fourth to Cappellini, who was the freshest man of all, and the last one to Rijkaard. After a few minutes, however, Frank came over to tell me: "Boss, the kid is shaking."

He had realised that Cappellini was too emotional. And so, I told Frank to take the fourth penalty and gave the fifth to Billy Costacurta.

The first man to step up to the spot was Dragan Stojkovic, who went low with his right and sent Giovanni Galli the wrong way. Our captain immediately replied to theirs. Baresi struck the ball hard with his right, and it went in under the crossbar.

Young Prosinecki also went with his right. Galli guessed correctly, but the penalty was angled away from him.

Van Basten moved towards the ball with that swan-like elegance, he barely touched it but it flew – hard and unsaveable – into the top-right corner. Perfect execution.

I had the sense that the whole Marakana had been frozen by this exhibition of confidence and technique. That included Savicevic, who took an uncertain run-up and hit a limp low shot straight down the middle. Galli dived to his left, but managed to block the ball with his legs.

Evani scored with a flat left-footed strike, easily wrong-footing Stojanovic. We were now in front, 4-3. All the pressure of those 120,000 people now shifted onto the shoulders of Mitar Mrkela, who betrayed his fear by slowing down in his run-up then hitting the ball flat, trying to minimise the risks. He ended up producing a timid, low shot which the excellent Giovanni Galli intercepted by diving to his right.

If Rijkaard scored, we were through. Frank, the man I wanted instead of Borghi…

I turned my back to the pitch; I didn't want to watch. Through the absolute silence of the Marakana, I heard the dull thud of the ball striking a post. The blood froze in my veins. But after hitting the woodwork, the ball rolled into the net. Rijkaard had hit the ball hard with his right-foot, sending it in the opposite direction.

I've never forgotten the sound of that post – a hymn to happiness. We were in the quarter-finals! I ran on to the pitch and hugged each of my players in turn. We had beaten Red Star, but also suffered injustice, violence, provocation. They'd spat in our faces, a policeman had set his wolfhound on Costacurta. And yet we'd been stronger than everything and everyone.

I found myself alongside a Milan superfan whom everyone called Ghadaffi – he really did look like the Libyan leader. I've no idea how he had managed to get on there. That bloke cost us a pretty hefty fine because the fans shouted from the terraces: "Welcome back, Ghadaffi!" and UEFA interpreted the chant as a political statement. To get the fine rescinded, we had to bring the pretend Ghadaffi in front of a UEFA panel and show them the resemblance.

Back in the dressing room, once the tension had dropped, we allowed ourselves a few smiles. Gullit, lying on the massage table, asked: "When's the next round of the

European Cup?" Tassotti, remembering all the little niggles (more or less serious) that Ruud had experienced since the start of the season, replied: "March. Do you think you'll be back by then?" It was only November.

I told Dr Monti how, when Donadoni went down, Van Basten had run to the bench screaming, "A doctor! A doctor!" We explained to him: "Monti's already on." But he insisted: "No, a doctor! A doctor!"

I needled Monti: "Some faith the Dutch lad has in you, Ginko!"

They'd put Donadoni in a hospital room with a bloke who had fallen from a third-floor window. To help Roberto quench his thirst, this kind man poured drops of orange juice into his mouth. Roberto was still struggling to open it.

The Red Star manager and Vasilijevic, the defender who had struck him, visited the hospital. Finally, a bit of sportsmanship.

Roberto always gave the absolute maximum in every minute of the match or training session. He gave the best possible interpretation of my concept of hard work and sense of duty. For this reason, his teammates called him 'Bone'. He never gave in. He was a hero. Not because he ended up in hospital with his head half smashed. He was a hero in the manner defined by Romain Rolland – the French writer who won the Nobel Prize for Literature. "A hero is someone who does what he can." I agree with this sentiment, and using it, I can say that I coached a team of heroes who then became Immortal.

The following day, before we left for Milan, the Red Star president and the mayor of Belgrade came to offer their congratulations and wish us luck for the rest of the tournament. They delivered a happy prophecy: "We're paying our respects to the future winners of the European

Cup." Silvio Berlusconi gifted Donadoni a painting worth a fortune.

Giovanni Galli, who saved two penalties, was one of the most celebrated figures in the aftermath, and rightly so. It wasn't easy being the goalkeeper in that Milan team. If I'm not mistaken, in my first year, he wasn't given a man-marks rating* in 16 of the 30 games he played. You might only face one shot per match, but when it came, you had to be ready to react. At the end of one of those games where he didn't get a rating, I offered my congratulations to Giovanni. He thought I was making fun of him. "But boss, I didn't make a single save."

I'd kept an eye on him for the full 90 minutes and he'd always been in the right position in respect of the ball – always active and concentrating.

Giovanni was an absolute gem of a boy and it was a real shame when he left Milan. In his last season, I alternated him with Andrea Pazagli, whom I'd signed because he was good at coming out.

While we're talking about No.1s, my first goalkeeper at Fusignano was called Pino Gemelli. He was 13 years older than me and had spent good time in Serie B and C with Livorno, Forlì and Ravenna. We won the league, but because Fusignano didn't pay players a single Lira, he signed for Voltana, a nearby village. In the Fusignano-Voltano derby, the referee awarded us a penalty. The player who stepped up to take it was Carles Balestra, who I thought was better than Paolo Maldini. Everyone laughed when I said that, but I wasn't joking. If Puskas was more dangerous

---

* The 'Pagelle' player ratings are an institution in Italian football reporting. When there is deemed to be insufficient evidence – like when a goalkeeper is not tested – the writer may choose not to give the player a mark

from 30m than a normal player from five, Balestra was more dangerous from 10m. A left-back, he scored 15-20 goals a season for me.

Gimelli was well aware of how his former teammate took his penalties, and so Carles, who was right-footed, struck the ball with his left to fool him. We won the derby.

Balestra's head was screwed on in a certain way. He'd end up banned for half the season. Once, we were top and about to play Sesto Imolese, who had eaten into our lead by five points and were now only a couple of lengths back, in second. We were missing three or four players – a full-on emergency. I said to Carles, "behave yourself, now".

Somebody in the crowd insulted him, he jumped on the safety netting and laid him out with a punch. Another time, he disappeared for a whole week. I phoned his wife and she replied: "Why are you asking me? He's not been home for three days."

But he was strong; he was my Puskas. When I went to Bellaria in the fourth division, I tried to take him with me. Before the trial, I had a good talk with him. "Listen, Carles. Behave yourself and work hard."

Off we went and he got into a fist fight with the Bellaria captain. Forget it. I still see him from time to time. He's had a thousand jobs and lives in Alfonsine.

While we're still on the subject of goalkeepers and unique personalities, at Cesena I had Sebastiano Rossi, who won the National Reserve League with me. One day, before he had even made it into the reserves, he came looking for me. I was in charge of the whole youth section, and he said: "Boss, I need to talk to you."

"No problem. Let's speak after training," I proposed.

"No, right now," he insisted.

"As you wish. What is it you want to tell me?"

"Boss, I can't play football anymore," he explained.

"Why not?"

"Because I've fallen in love."

"You do know you can do both those things, play and be in love?" I said.

"Really, you can? In that case, that's what I'll do. Thanks," he replied and walked off.

I brought eight players with me from Cesena to Rimini, but not Seba Rossi, who moved to Forlì. In the first two league games he played brilliantly and everyone was talking about him. In the third, Seba made a save – perhaps one-handed, as he liked to do – and passed the ball round his back before kicking it out. The ball slipped from his grasp, their centre-forward pounced and scored.

In 1990, I brought him to Milan, paying very little by way of a transfer fee. I recommended to the club that they kept him for no more than a couple of years. "For two seasons, he'll manage fine and behave himself. Then he'll smash everything up."

Instead, Milan kept him for 12 years.

After the Battle of Belgrade and our performance at the Marakana, suspicions were raised about doping. But our doping was mental: ideas were what pushed us to be running forwards, and hard work was what allowed us to do so.

For years, a lot of people spoke about the luck we'd had with the fog. My view is that if the fog hadn't come, there might have been a different story that time round, but we would definitely have won a European Cup at some point.

There hasn't been real fog in Fusignano for 20 years. I mean the proper stuff: the thick, old-fashioned kind that hides everything in a flash, leaving you unable to see your hand in front of your face. One November morning in 1991, I'd gone for a run beside a riding school that sits a kilometre away from my house. In that spot, during the Second World War, 10 partisans had been killed. I used to go running there quite often, because there was a nice little gravel path. On this particular day, a thick fog closed in and you couldn't see more than five metres. I really liked the atmosphere. I was completely alone, immersed in peace and an absolute emptiness that gave me great serenity. Via the radio I had with me, I learned that Azeglio Vicini, the Italy manager, had been sacked. From February of that year, I'd had an agreement with the Federation that I would be the man to replace him.

When I told Berlusconi that I was leaving Milan, he did everything in his power to push me towards Real Madrid. He was terrified that I would end up at Juventus. He even offered two billion lire to convince me – more than my annual salary at Milan. I was disappointed and upset – those sums did not make any sense.

I decided to leave after the second European Cup. I no longer had gastritis, but I was profoundly disillusioned by injustice, because we had been tricked out of a league title. Everyone saw that Alemao had been ordered to stay down in Bergamo, even though the coin hadn't really hurt him*.

---

* Milan were a point ahead of Napoli with four games to go when Maradona's men played Atalanta in Bergamo. With 15 minutes to play, the score was 0-0. Alemao, the Napoli midfielder, was struck on the top of the head by a coin thrown from the Atalanta *curva*. He seemed relatively unharmed but was encouraged by the Napoli physio, Salvatore Carmando, to come off. The Italian federation had recently introduced a rule whereby if a player had to be removed due to fan behaviour, that player's team would be awarded a win. With Milan drawing in Bologna, Napoli were now level on points amid huge controversy

We played better than Napoli and it was right and proper that we won the scudetto, even if we'd arrived at the end of the season short of breath. We had won the Intercontinental Cup and European Supercup and we were also in the Coppa Italia final. Berlusconi made the error of talking about a Grand Slam. It's something you should never mention – doing so brings worse luck than Verona.

We were knackered by the time we went to play Verona in the Bentegodi. I've discovered things that went on in the background to that match which I'm not in a position to recount. Verona won 2-1, with the referee, Concetto Lo Bello, sending off Van Basten, Rijkaard, Costacurta and yours truly. We finished the game with eight players and Napoli won the league.

I went to see Berlusconi and offered my resignation. The president didn't accept, and sent me on a 10-day holiday. To convince me to stay on, he even arranged a helicopter trip – I was just a passenger.

Years later, when I was a Real Madrid director, Alemao – who by now was an agent – came to our offices to offer us one of his players. I introduced him to Emilio Butragueno and Ramon Martinez, who headed up our youth section and was in charge of scouting. "This man cost me a league title," I said.

Alemao, clearly embarrassed, explained: "I carried out an instruction. It was a mistake. But I suffered more than anyone because it ruined my career. I believe I was a good player, but now I'm only remembered for that coin."

Regardless, we didn't buy the player he was offering.

The Battle of Belgrade probably cost us a title as well. That match stayed in our collective memory as an absolute peak of suffering, to the extent it became legendary.

I remember Costacurta coming to me one day during

World Cup 94, where the climactic conditions were gruelling and we encountered a series of problems. Billy said: "Boss, every game here is a Belgrade."

We came back from Yugoslavia exhausted, psychologically spent after so much tension. We then went through the most difficult period of the whole season, where the league title was at stake and my position began to get precarious once again. For the second year in a row, my panettone was at risk of disappearing*.

---

* Panettone is a very popular Christmas food in Italy. Managers who are not expected to survive until the New Year are said to be at risk of "not eating their panettone"

TRAP'S WHISTLE

Between playing Atalanta at home in the sixth round of the championship on November 20, 1988, and going to Cesena in the 12th round on January 8, we played seven league matches and lost four – double the amount of defeats in the whole of the previous campaign. We drew twice and won only once – against Lecce in the eighth round.

At the start of that run, we were a single point behind Giovanni Trapattoni's Inter. By the end of it, we were 10 points back. We had ripped the shield* off our own breasts.

The first warning siren was heard in that self-same game against Atalanta at the San Siro a few days after the Battle of Belgrade. We were missing Donadoni and Gullit, and Cappellini started. We went behind to a Baresi own goal, then equalised late on, courtesy of a great strike

* The *scudetto* emblem worn by the reigning champions

from Rijkaard. In the very last minute, they had a corner. Poor Emiliano Mondonico, the Atalanta manager, was gesticulating at his players to stay back, because he was afraid of the counter-attack.

Our penalty area emptied of black and blue jerseys and only Valter Bonacina remained. He was the smallest player on the park, barely coming up to Rijkaard's hip. He scored with a header.

In terms of awareness and concentration, we just weren't there. Not even in the 90th minute. Indeed, in my log-book I wrote:

> *We're paying dearly for the many absentees but even more costly is the lack of humility and will to win compared to last year. This creates carelessness, as shown by the goal we gave away at the end.*

After the 1-0 derby loss to Inter on December 11 (Aldo Serena was the scorer) I went a lot harder:

> *If this is good enough for you, let's carry on. We'll have a lot of success, I'm sure. What's happening is a complete betrayal of the club, me, the fans and everyone who identifies with our footballing ideology. Those people attracted by the new type of game we were offering. We're suffering from a clear drop in desire, attentiveness and determination. We're doing too many things carelessly. We're soft in just about every aspect: pressing, marking, speed.*
>
> *Your image, as well as mine, has been abruptly downsized. Enough is enough. We need to look forwards. Milan can't have spent all this money on*

players, back-room staff etc to then disappoint in such a manner. Please don't think it's just a case of getting a few injured players back – we need to rediscover our game and our mentality.

If this team doesn't have a few things, like pressing and pace, it loses 50% of its potential. The teams I've coached have always fought to win, or they've won when they've had anger and character.

Inter, who after that derby were two points clear of Napoli and seven clear of us, were on the way to winning what they'd call the 'record-breaking *scudetto*'. They were a strong team who played a very Italian style of football. Giovanni Trapattoni had excellent knowledge and rich experience of this approach and was always an extraordinary individual.

This was our traditional football and he did it well, with kindness, empathy and excellent man-management. He was an extraordinary tactician.

Here's what Inter invented for us: because Milan control the midfield, we'll drop Lothar Matthaus back between the centre-backs and ask him to hit long balls to Nicola Berti and the strikers.

Tactics, not strategy. I repeat: Tactics are about trying to take advantage of an opposition weakness and waiting for them to make a mistake. A strategy is a positive plan of action to carry out.

Among their tactics was narrowing the pitch. In the years where Trapattoni and I were both coaching in Milan, the San Siro pitch was a kind of accordion. When Milan were at home, it expanded, because we needed as much pitch as possible to attack. When Inter were at home, it contracted, because they needed as little pitch as possible to defend. A

UEFA delegate once cottoned on and asked us to explain the parallel lines that could be made out further in from the touchline.

Only once in my life have I adopted a tactical approach. We were playing against Fiorentina in the neutral venue of Perugia and were losing 2-0. They'd stuck Dunga on Ancelotti, making sure to man-mark him wherever he went on the pitch.

I called Carlo over and instructed him: "Go and play on the flank and don't move from there." Dunga duly followed him, abandoning the middle of the field. We recovered and won 3-2.

That was the one and only time in my career, because tactics without strategy are for losers. If the opposition played their right-back really deep, I wouldn't push my left-back really high to take advantage. I wasn't going to change our game – that is, our strength – to lean on the weaknesses of others.

One day Gullit asked me: "Boss, why don't we go long to the strikers every now and then so that we get a little rest?"

I replied: "Because if you do it once, you'll do it twice the next game, and three times the next one after that. We'll end up not playing with the ball at all."

I have huge respect for Trapattoni, not least because he has a track record which makes plain his worth. I really like him: he's a fair, upstanding human being.

I do envy him one thing: his whistle. At home, my daughter Federica would always say: "Daddy, you're not a real manager – you can't whistle."

I'd explain: "I try, but they don't hear me."

That's why I used the megaphone.

That lost derby pushed my panettone even further away. I

still managed to eat it, but after two less than brilliant draws against Torino and Sampdoria, we collapsed against Cesena. They beat us 1-0 thanks to a goal from Hans Holmqvist, the Swede.

The home crowd sang: "Your seat is about to explode/ Dear Arrigo/ Your seat is about to explode!"

Marked in the Smemoranda is the high point of my disappointment and resentment.

> *A team with too little will to win. We are champions of presumptuousness, feeling sated, carelessness and slackness*
> *Our game is poorly constructed – everyone is playing for themselves, rather than thinking about their teammates, the rhythm of the game and movement off the ball.*
> *We're missing easy chances and conceding goals worthy of the FIGC Investigations Unit. We should be ashamed. We're stealing our wages. We can't go on like this. We're soft and floppy and only become more decisive when we go behind. We're full of fear. The other teams aren't playing well, but they all have a grit, an anger and a decisiveness that we've lost. We're unlucky because we do not deserve good fortune. At the moment, we're loose cannons – only a few players are trying to move in tandem with the others, and then the chaos overwhelms them.*

No half-hearted bludgeonings here…

The list of things to improve, noted in my log-book, confirms my livid state of mind.

> *Switches of play; dribbling; players criss-crossing to*

switch positions; overlapping without the ball; give and-go's; timing; interceptions; shots; crossing; tackling; pressing; rapid counter-attacks, changes of rhythm

With me in this kind of mood, the team understood they wouldn't find a session of thermal baths and massage waiting for them at Milanello. Indeed, here is the schedule for our first training day after Cesena:

10 minutes of stretching and technical work: in two 15x15m squares, ball carrying and dribbling.
10 minutes of muscle-building exercise: 4x8 reps of squats plus jumping to increase leg strength
Technical work in team units
Five minutes of precision shooting with one-twos.
10 minutes of possession games, 8v8, two-touch, on a 40x40m pitch
Shots with dribbling
10 minutes of 8v5 half-pitch game
14 minutes of interval running: one minute hard, followed by one-minute lower intensity
Total duration of session: One hour 20 minutes, with minimal recovery between exercises to keep intensity high

The following day's morning session:

10 minutes of stretching
10 minutes of 7v7 hand game, on a 20x20m pitch
6 minutes of skipping
5 minutes of 3x back-and-forth shuttle runs
5 minutes of technical work

10 minutes of uphill running; 6x30m with 50 seconds of recovery time and 4x50m with one minute of recovery time
10 minutes of upper body and abdominal strength work
10 minutes of work with the strikers

Afternoon session:

10 minutes of 7x7 possession game on a 40x25m pitch
15 minutes of 8v4 possession game on a 35x35m pitch, counting the balls per minute intercepted by the team of four
20 minutes of crossing and two-on-ones on the flank
10 minutes of 7v7 game on a 50x40m pitch, unlimited touches. This will keep Van Basten happy.
15 minutes of 7v7 on full pitch, pressing drill

Double session the next day, too.

After our defeat by Cesena, Aldo Biscardi said on his *Processo** TV show that I would be sacked. Galliani summoned me to the club office, so I called Natale Bianchedi, my trusty scout whom I'd sent to Bremen to study Werder, our next European Cup opponent.

"Natale," I warned him, "there's an ill-wind blowing here. I'd advise you to pack up your things and return immediately – otherwise you might have to pay the hotel bill yourself. Soon enough Milan might not be covering

---

* *Il Processo di Biscardi* was a ground-breaking football talk show that ran on Italian TV from 1980-2016

our expenses." In reality, the discussion with Galliani was to be about renewing my contract. As a club, Milan were anything but daft, just as I'd suspected the previous time. That run of league defeats had left my popularity at its lowest point, and so they could negotiate from a position of strength. I gambled big, but Galliani struck back: "Arrigo, you can't ask for double every time we sit down."

They offered me a sum of 100 million lire lower than what I'd asked for. I replied: "Fine, I accept your offer. But if we win the European Cup, you give me three times the difference."

They accepted. After being beaten by Cesena, it wasn't easy to imagine Milan as European champions. But I knew the tables would soon turn, due to the usual reason: ideas and hard work.

The ideas were lodged in our heads – we couldn't have forgotten them. Those diary pages overflowing with drills show how hard we'd worked and, sooner or later, hard work always pays off.

Even on January 12 I wrote:

> *Good session today, real grit. This could be the turning point.*

Two days later, after we had beaten Como 4-0 at the San Siro, I was able to confirm:

> *Good result. We're back on the right track. The important thing now is to continue on it. The team still isn't in the best physical, technical or tactical condition, but they're playing with more grit and enthusiasm. We're also being more aware*

and showing greater humility.

Gullit had started and scored. Van Basten had found the net after barely three minutes. Virdis, as usual, came up with a goal too. We were coming back to ourselves as we prepared to head back into Europe.

The same conclusion was reached by three excellent French coaches whom I hosted at Milano for 10 days that January: Luis Fernandez, Gerard Houllier and Arsene Wenger. They watched our sessions and before leaving, said to me: "We've never seen a team work so hard. You'll be the next European champions."

Berlusconi had not appreciated the visit of the three Frenchmen. He thought it was wrong for me to give away my secrets by letting others watch my sessions. I explained to him that they wouldn't achieve the same results simply by copying what they had seen. The true secret lay in the details, in the constant attention to time and space. Because a second's delay in a pass, or a metre of difference in positioning can compromise the whole operation. These things need to be worked on continuously in training so that players memorise them exactly. They then become instinctive, automatic. If a coach doesn't have the awareness to work on these things, copying a drill won't be of any use.

Cesare Prandelli, for example, is brilliant at carrying out this kind of fine-tuning during training sessions. Antonio Conte, too. He's an excellent coach who just needs to have more self-belief.

We were through the worst. We were beginning to flower once more as spring drew closer.

On February 18, we won 2-0 away to Fiorentina with

goals from Colombo and Ancelotti. Another confirmation was recorded in the Smemoranda: *We're on the right track.* However, given that there was optimism in the air and the team was receptive, I made a note of 12 things to improve. Not one, 12…

I surpassed myself after the following game. The boys put six past Pescara and I wrote: *Must improve our finishing.*

Either way, we were ready for Werder Bremen, who we would play in Germany on March 1 with a full-blown emergency in our defence. Giovanni Galli had one hand all bandaged up, Tassotti had inflammation in his knee, Baresi had bumps and bruises and Maldini was suspended. Yet as we weren't going to man the barricades, but attack like we always did, the problem was only relative. I played Costacurta at left-back with Rijkaard in the middle of the backline.

The Monday before the game, Luigi Berlusconi – the president's father – died. Franco Baresi, our captain, phoned to offer the team's condolences and we wore black armbands against Werder.

I well-remembered how German people spoke about Italians when I travelled there with my father to sell shoes. As well as Werder, I was playing against those prejudices: pizza, mafia, mandolin and catenaccio.

It was raining and an icy wind blew. The pitch was in a terrible state. To progress, we would need a real show of character, an ability to withstand suffering, not least because Otto Rehhagel was an excellent coach. His Werder Bremen knew how to press, they moved in an organised fashion, and they had grit, legs and pride. In the first round, they'd lost 3-0 away to Dynamo Berlin then scored five at home. Up front, they had a fearsome duo: Frank Neubarth, tall and dangerous in the air, and Karl-Heinz Riedle, the future

Lazio man, who was small and fast.

Their defence was anchored by the Norwegian giant, Rune Bratseth. Werder went to war with us for 90 minutes in the middle of a storm on that dreadful pitch.

That night, I recalled the words of Bruno Pesaola, the former Napoli manager, who once promised in an eve-of-match press conference: "We'll attack them from start to finish." The following day, however, his team stayed holed up in defence. At the end of the game, the press asked him about his pre-match promise and he replied: "Our opponents stole our idea."

Here, too, Werder stole our idea, but we still managed to score a perfectly good goal against them. In the 27th minute, Donadoni takes a corner, Rijkaard gets his head to the ball and a defender stops it with his chest on the line. He tries to head the ball away, but it hits the post and goes in. The defender is in despair, holding his head in his hands, while Oliver Reck, the goalkeeper, dives into the net and pushes the ball out. Quite incredibly, the Portuguese referee, Jose Rosa dos Santos – a little bald bloke with a big black moustache – waves play on. Another theft, just like in Belgrade!

Bruno Pizzul remembered that immediately during the live RAI TV broadcast: "Goal! Goal! Goal! It's a goal! It's a goal! Goal!" He repeated it six times. Another 'clear and obvious' strike that we were denied. Scandalous.

To tell the truth, the referee, perhaps driven by remorse, then ruled out a Werder goal for an apparent shove on Giovanni Galli that appeared quite soft. Van Basten, who wasn't having a great night, passed up two excellent chances. The first one he hit straight at the keeper. With the second, having been picked out by a brilliant Donadoni pass, he managed to round Reck and get away a shot, but it was too weak. Bratseth the giant managed to get back in time and clear the ball off the line on the slide.

An extremely hard-fought game finished 0-0. Naturally, we were furious. Costacurta revealed that Dos Santos had apologised for the error. Galliani was livid. "Man of the Match? The referee, along with the right-side linesman."

I said: "I've asked Ramaccioni if by some chance they'd changed the rules. It's now clear that we are playing to our own special ones. For us, getting the ball over the line is not enough for a goal. Three pieces of evidence prove a case and we're already at two. As I'm not stupid, I think I've understood what's going on."

I'd understood that Silvio Berlusconi had had a brilliant idea in the shape of his European Super League project, but that it had been an error to make it public. The existing national leagues would lose prestige while UEFA would miss out on a large amount of money. Perhaps we were already beginning to pay the price.

In my log-book, I made a list of reflections that would inform the second leg:

> *Very difficult game against a team full of grit, strength, awareness, pressing, speed and resistance. Werder were quicker and more aggressive than us. We need to avoid being hit on the counter-attack and must remain very compact. We need to avoid sideways passing. We must move the ball quickly and not just wait for it in a stationary position. It's really important that players shrug off markers when they don't have the ball. Space is our home.*

I knew that the Germans would put up a real fight at the

San Siro. To reach the semi-finals, we would need to play like the real Milan.

11 v 0

European Cup
Quarter-final, second leg
Milan 1 Werder Bremen 0

Three days before the return leg against Werder Bremen, we played Juventus in a dress rehearsal that made us feel good about ourselves. We put in a sparkling performance and won 4-0. Mannari came on late and scored twice. Van Basten was drawing a blank after missing one too many chances in Bremen. He was the guy who we needed to pull us through back at the San Siro.

That Wednesday, the stadium was packed with more than 70,000 fans, all ready to push us into the semi-finals. I had Paolo Maldini back and Costacurta was on the bench.

It turned out to be another hard-fought, tetchy match on a heavy pitch. The synopsis I recorded in my log-book was honest and up front:

Decent performance, excellent result.

We didn't play as well as we had against Juve: our moves weren't as fluid, which had something to do with the quality of the Germans' press. And I must acknowledge that the penalty which decided the outcome was non-existent.

Half an hour in, Gullit went long to Colombo, who crossed from the right wing. A lovely caress from the outside of Van Basten's boot set Donadoni free, and as the midfielder turned to shoot he came into contact with a defender and went down in the box. The contact did not appear to warrant a foul, but the referee pointed to the spot. Van Basten converted with a hard right-footed shot into the bottom corner. A flawless, ice-cool finish.

We were made to suffer right until the finish. Colombo, Donadoni and Gullit all wasted big chances, keeping alive the hopes of the Germans, who never gave up. When the Scottish referee George Smith eventually blew for full-time, their goalkeeper, Reck, lashed out at him and was sent off. This time it was Werder Bremen who were livid.

Otto Rehhagel said: "We were beaten by the referee alone."

Paul Breitner, the former West Germany full-back who lost the 1982 World Cup final to Italy, was in the San Siro stands that night and spoke of a "scandal" afterwards. Tasso, always the height of wisdom, concluded: "The referee gave us back the goal they stole from us in Bremen."

What was certain was that in the two quarter-final matches, we played better than Werder and deserved more than them.

The draw in Geneva pitted us against Real Madrid. Here I was in the European Cup, against the team that I'd dreamed about as a kid, watching Di Stefano, Puskas and Gento in those white shirts on Lorenzo Zagonari's TV set. My big moment had arrived.

Ruud Gullit expressed a thought that I believe was

shared by many: "It's a shame to be playing each other so soon, because this would have been a worthy final."

In my own initial comments, I played it cute, saying something like: "I'm pleased to have avoided Galatasaray, because we know less about them."

Berlusconi was on more or less the same lines. "We've already beaten them twice. As Milan president, I say we're better than Real Madrid. As a Milan fan, I say we're twice as good."

In reality, we would be up against a brilliant team who were about to win their fourth straight La Liga title, and who in the last four years had won two UEFA Cups. They were desperate to lift the European Cup for the first time in 23 years – having won the first five editions of the competition, they believed it was a trophy that belonged to them and needed to be brought home.

They played positive, optimistic, attacking football and had great champions who were famous throughout the world: Manolo Sanchis, Michel, Bernd Schuster, Martin Vasquez, Emilio Butragueno, Hugo Sanchez…

Our strategy of approaching the European Cup by playing Real twice at the end of the previous season and the start of this one certainly helped reduce the emotional impact, especially when we stepped out at the cathedral of the Bernabeu, which we had already desecrated thanks to Mannari.

Leo Beenhakker, Madrid's Dutch coach, had a pleasant surprise in store for me. On the day of the draw in Geneva, he boarded Galliani's private jet, touched down in Milan and came to see me. We shared a joke.

"This time, you won't come to our house and win 3-0," he advised. "This time, 2-0 will be enough," I reassured him.

On April 1, the day of my 46th birthday, we had our

dress rehearsal away to Atalanta. The only one missing was Gullit, who was on a course of antibiotics for a bout of flu. I put him on in the second half, with Virdis starting.

Atalanta went ahead straight away through Eligio Nicolini, but we pulled level thanks to Evani and won when Rijkaard scored. At the end, Berlusconi revealed with pride: "Before the match, I told Frank to shoot more often." By this point, Borghi was a distant memory.

The newspapers were always debating whether midfield or defence was Rijkaard's best position. Every time he went back to Holland, we would see quotes that he was dissatisfied or even angry. Ancelotti had also made public his own thoughts: "I'd never move him from the midfield."

I knew fine well that Frank preferred to play as a midfielder – we'd spoken about it often – but at that moment I needed him as a fulcrum, alongside Baresi, and he always took on that role with admirable discipline. He never came to me to moan, and I never heard of him making a fuss with anyone else. Frank Rijkaard is a true gentleman, an utterly splendid person.

In 1990, he went through a tough period due to personal problems. That tension was writ large at the World Cup in Italy, when he spat in Rudi Voller's face. That wasn't him.

I asked to see him and spoke clearly. "Frank, if you're an honest man, go to the club offices, explain that you can no longer give us what you did before, and request a transfer."

He got over this momentary crisis and went back to being the splendid player he always was.

In 1992, however, even though Milan were offering him a stack of cash to stay, he explained that he was feeling home-sick for Ajax and would be leaving Italy at the end of the season. I was national team manager by then, but Frank knew that I often had lunch in a certain Milanese restaurant close to via San Carpoforo, where I had a house. He left a letter for me at the restaurant.

It read: "Boss, I'm an honest man. I went to the club offices and explained I can longer give what I did before. I'm going back to Holland. Thanks for everything." He hadn't forgotten what I'd told him two years previously. These were the great men who made my Milan team great.

The match at the Bernabeu was preceded by a fever of anticipation that infected everyone including the Pope. John Paul II let it be known that he would be watching on TV. Gianni Agnelli, the Juventus owner, phoned Berlusconi to tell him he would be at the game, but then a last-minute commitment forced him to pull out.

On the eve of the match, our president showed all his irrepressible optimism. "If luck is on our side, we'll win, and it won't be close." It wasn't enough for him to win; he wanted to thrash Real Madrid on their own patch.

By contrast, Ramon Mendoza, the Real president, was a big believer in the assistance of Saint Gemma Galgani. He always carried a prayer card with her picture that the widow of the mythical Santiago Bernabeu had gifted him.

In football, even the most unlikely figures are superstitious. Nils Liedholm, for example. Everyone thought of 'The Baron' as a very rational Nordic type, a master of good sense, but Ancelotti told me of how once, when they worked together at Roma, he had picked up Liedholm's jacket by mistake and found all sorts in the pocket. A horn-shaped pendant, a rabbit foot…

I also heard about his superstitions when I first arrived at Milan. He was convinced, for example, that a certain kit store worker brought him bad luck, and as such he never wanted to see him at the stadium before a game. When we played the Baron's Roma, I ordered that self-same worker to stand in front of the dressing rooms, knowing that sooner or later he would run into Liedholm.

Nils saw him and said: "You've been told to stand here, right?"

Another time, I bought a bunch of flowers and told the same worker to give them to the Baron.

In the January of my first year at Milan, we lost away to Ascoli in the Coppa Italia. A month later, we went back there in the league and, because I remember everything, I noticed that nobody was sitting in the same place in the dressing room that they'd had for the cup match.

I said to Gullit: "Ruud, is even someone like you superstitious?"

Naturally, he wanted to show that he was above it all. "No, boss. It's just that I came in last and the spot I had last time was already taken."

Personally speaking, I was more wary of co-incidence than superstition. I'd realised, for example, that the number 17 brought me good luck and that whenever that meteoropath Van Basten paid me a compliment, it was wise to touch wood, because something negative always happened soon after.

For example, that time he came back from Holland and told me that Milan were playing much better than his national team, we lost to Lazio at the San Siro the following weekend without them even having a proper shot on goal. We'd pummelled them from start to finish. Maldini scored an own goal with a backpass from midfield. Paolo Di Canio was almost apologetic at the finish: "Boss, I don't know how we managed to win. We couldn't even get over the halfway line."

When we signed Van Basten, I consulted Professor Silvagni, an astrological expert from Fusignano who could predict someone's destiny from the date and time of their birth. I showed him Marco's, explaining that I was talking about a footballer but not telling him who. He looked at the details and declared: "He will have a short career, full of injuries."

After the Second World War, to earn a living Professor Silvagni organised shows at Marina di Ravenna on the Adriatic Coast. He would have his assistant bury him on the beach then stay there under the sand for hours. The problem was that his assistant, like almost everyone in Fusignano, loved to gamble. One day, when he was stood there with the cards in his hand, he went pale and shouted: "The professor is soaking!" He should have pulled him out of the sand half an hour earlier and the tide had already come in. They saved the poor professor in the nick of time.

While compliments from Marco brought bad luck, I'd noticed that encountering horses had the opposite effect. One time, when we were on the bus taking us to the Olimpico for a crucial 1994 World Cup qualifier against Scotland, I spied some horses in the Roman countryside through the window. A good sign. I looked out the other side and saw a flock of sheep. Onwards went the bus. I tried desperately to find some other horses but all I saw was sheep. A nightmare. Just as well the game went against these negative omens.

Another time, before a different national team match, Gigia Riva – our team manager – found me on the ground doing push-ups. We ended up winning, and before each subsequent match, he insisted on me doing more push-ups prior to taking my seat on the bench.

We flew to Madrid on a DC9 plane. It was a first away trip for Adriana Fossa, the Venezuelan model whom Paolo Maldini went on to marry in 1994. Every now and then, I spoke with the players' wives, in particular Anna Galli (Giovanni's better half, who was friends with my Giovanna), Luisa Ancelotti and Maura Baresi. Occasionally I'd also organise team dinners to which wives and girlfriends were invited. It was another way of ensuring harmony and togetherness in the group.

For the 1989 Intercontinental Cup final, I went overboard and showed I was a true progressive: I invited all the women to Tokyo. Silvano Ramaccioni, our team manager and a wise, wise man, wasn't particularly enamoured with the prospect. He told me with a real sense of worry: "Arrigo, in eight days they'll destroy two years of hard work."

Indeed, this was no straightforward away trip. We would be in Japan for 10 days and the women had split off into twos – there was a risk that likes and dislikes would be formed and that in the space of a week, a war could break out.

I had sent Italo Galbiati to spy on Madrid's final training session. He reported back that, while Beenhakker spoke, a lot of players had been laughing and joking among themselves. A good sign – for us.

Madrid appeared very confident, but in reality they were harbouring doubts, and not just because of the two friendly defeats they had suffered against us. As Butragueno would reveal to me years later, the spy that Beenhakker sent to study us had come back with his head spinning. He didn't have much to report. It had been his misfortune to have turned up on a day when I ran one of our 11 v 0 sessions. No opposition and no ball either.

If Giovanni Galli turned to the right and looked like launching the imaginary ball in that direction, the right-back moved closer to him, while the left-back headed forward and every other player moved in symphony with their teammates. I would shout the name of the player in possession, and the whole team would move in synchrony, as if it was a single organism controlled by one brain. If I yelled "man on!", it meant that the player in possession had an opponent right on his coattails. The nearest teammate then had to run over to offer himself for a pass, not go deep in anticipation of a long ball.

What gave us strength were those automatisms, those internalised understandings that had been made instinctive by two years of work. Ideas and hard work – that's what it always comes back to. What gave us strength, courage and optimism was our game.

Gullit reiterated this to Ancelotti – his roommate – on the morning of the match. Ruud woke up and found Carlo right beside his bed, hands on hips and a harsh expression on his face. "I really want to know how you do it – I've watched you all night and you slept like a baby!"

Gullit, rubbing his eyes, struggled to make sense of the situation. "What's up with you, Carlo? What's happened?"

"What's happened is that tonight we're playing Real Madrid! At the Bernabeu, their ground!" Ancelotti exclaimed. "And you're sleeping soundly, as if it was nothing."

"Of course I'm sleeping soundly! Why do you care about Real Madrid? We're much stronger than them," Ruud replied. "When I play for Milan, I feel invincible. It doesn't matter if we're up against Avellino, Atalanta or Real Madrid. I have fun. Our game brings me joy and I always feel like we can win. In fact, I win even before the game kicks off. The opposition look at us and already understand that we're stronger than them. Tonight in the Bernabeu tunnel, the same thing will happen, Carlo. They'll look us in the eye and we'll start to win there and then."

It was with the heart of Ruud Gullit that we stepped out to play Real Madrid on the evening of April 5, 1989. More than 90,000 fans were packed inside the imposing Bernabeu. Twenty-two TV stations showed the game live: the whole world was watching us.

MILAN AREN'T ITALIAN

European Cup
Semi-final, first leg
Real Madrid 1 Milan 1

We have the kick-off. The ball goes back, we hit it long and a red and black tide sweeps, tight and inexorable, towards the Real Madrid goal. All night, we press and attack with our whole team, from the first minute until the last.

People who didn't know us weren't expecting it. They'd noticed we didn't concede many goals, and they knew we were Italian, so they thought we must be a team built on defence. Instead, the first chance of the match fell to Paolo Maldini, our left-back. The cross for Van Basten's equaliser was supplied by Tassotti, our right-back. It was Franco Baresi who played the ball to Donadoni that allowed Gullit to slip his marker in the build-up to the goal that was wrongly disallowed. Rijkaard broke out repeatedly and covered the whole pitch. That was my defence.

In fairness, Leo Beenhakker, who'd studied us closely, had sounded the alarm on the eve of the match. "Be aware: Milan aren't Italian." Just like in that last training session, they hadn't listened to him. At the end of the game, a bewildered Emilio Butragueno explained: "I've spent my whole life at Real. I've been here since I was a kid. I've never seen a team come to the Bernabeu and be as dominant as Milan were tonight."

It was that game which made us well-known and also gave us definitive proof of our own strength. The world looking in on the Bernabeu bore witness to something new. I could repeat a comment made about me by Chicco Evani in an interview: "Arrigo was so far ahead that, if he turned round, he saw the future."

That Milan team was so far ahead, so different, that Real didn't know what to do with us. They were caught offside 27 times. Every time Martin Vasquez or Ricardo Gallego tried to set something up, they found our men pressing en-masse. Our defenders attacked from all sides. The Spaniards suffered our dominance for the full 90 minutes, and the scoreline flattered them.

AsI said, the first chance fell to Maldini. We had a great game, but also great champions capable of carrying it out to the highest standards, even in the worst weather conditions. Paolo was the perfect example of how intimidating the charisma and personality of a world-class player can be. Butragueno once told me that every time Real played Milan, Michel never slept the night before, because he was thinking about the duel with Maldini that awaited him. In reality, I reckon Paolo had the odd thought about Michel as well, because these were two truly fantastic talents.

When I was working for Real, I went to watch a young Sergio Ramos playing for Sevilla many times. I wanted to bring him to Madrid at all costs, but his price tag was prohibitive: €25m in 2005. Our president, Florentino Perez, was not convinced about spending so much money on a full-back. To persuade him, I used Paolo's name. I said: "Mr President. Buy him and I'll turn him into the new Maldini." The prospect of having a Paolo Maldini on his hands made Florentino open his wallet. Sergio Ramos is a warrior with a steely personality, but I've seen him come over all emotional and shrink in the presence of Paolo, whom he venerates with an absolute respect.

In a recent interview, Maldini called me "a visionary" and told how at Milan, I'd caused him nightmares. I sent him a text, saying: "Dear Paolo, if I caused you nightmares, I'm sorry and ask for your forgiveness."

He replied: "Boss, it's only thanks to those nightmares that I learned what football is."

That night at the Bernabeu, Paolo – who had been through a tough period but had returned to the peak of his powers – was one of Real Madrid's nightmares. Up in the stands, his father Cesare was sat next to the Italy manager, Azeglio Vicini.

After Maldini's chance, Van Basten had three. We were well on top, but not managing to score. Gullit wasn't in the best condition and, as so often happens in football, we paid the price for failing to make our dominance count.

Real went ahead in the 41st minute. At a corner, Manuel Sanchis miskicked but Baresi was a yard behind the line of defenders who pushed out. Hugo Sanchez, who was thus onside, finished acrobatically before celebrating with his customary somersault. The Mexican was a brilliant attacker with a pedigree goalscorer's instinct. Before bearing down on goal, he would always do this little movement in the 'D' which tended to open up the space for him to strike. Without the ball, however, he contributed almost nothing. There was simply no comparison between him and Van Basten.

After the first-half performance we'd given, going in behind was an absolute injustice. But we went back out unworried, determined to impose our game once more with the conviction that it would soon pay off, as always.

Sure enough, halfway through the second period we equalised, but the linesman ruled it out for a completely non-existent offside. After Belgrade and Bremen, here was the third piece of evidence that proved the case! Baresi went long to Donadoni, who crossed low to the middle of the box. Gullit, who turned it in, was not only behind the ball, but had a white jersey in front of him! The offside call was quite incredible, but we didn't relent even in the face of such injustice and finally, with 10 minutes to go, we reaped the rewards of our dominance.

Tassotti made ground on the right before putting in an imperfect cross that was just behind his man. To claim it, Van Basten had to take a step towards the middle of the pitch, dive, corkscrew his body in mid-air and head the ball with a brilliant twist of his neck. The sight was an absolute marvel that none of us will ever forget. The ball hit the underside of the bar, bounced off the back of Francisco Buyo, the Real goalkeeper, and went over the line. Buyo threw himself into the middle of the net to attempt a miraculous recovery and in that split-second, a lot of people would have been thinking about the 'clear and obvious' goals which weren't signed off by the officials in Belgrade and Bremen. But fortunately this time, the Swedish referee Erik Fredriksson pointed to the centre circle and the scoreline was 1-1.

Silvio Berlusconi, wearing an elegant fedora and white scarf, complained about the referee. "For a moment, I thought he was going to chalk off Van Basten's goal," but being on the receiving end of so many compliments had him visibly radiant. The whole world had admired his Milan.

The following day, the Spanish newspaper *AS* ran a headline of 'Footballing lesson at the Bernabeu'. "It was a joy to watch Ancelotti win dozens of balls and Baresi lead the defence out from the back."

'Joy' was the right word to describe our football. Another Spanish paper – I can't remember which – spoke about us as if they'd borne witness to a Martian invasion. "A truly marvellous team passed through the Bernabeu last night." They calculated that we'd spent two thirds of the match – a whole hour – in the Real Madrid half.

Naturally, I found these comments flattering, but I would have preferred to read them after the second leg. Regardless, in my log-book I noted my satisfaction, along with a few reservations and the list of aspects to improve which I always gave when things were going well.

> *Good game – excellent at times. Scoreline harsh on us. Good individual performances from defenders and midfielders. Strikers less good, particularly Gullit To improve: the strikers' depth, how the forward players attack space. The team needs to be even more compact Too many pointless, sideways passes.*

I also wrote myself a reminder: "Get hold of two tickets." Obviously, somebody had already requested them for the second leg.

Speaking to the media the day after the match in Madrid, Berlusconi was a lot more critical than I'd been in the pages of the Smemoranda. "The Milan we saw in the Bernabeu was an excellent boxer without a knock-out punch. If we'd had Butragueno and Sanchez, we would have won."

These were seemingly harsh, even ungenerous words, but there was a precise intention behind them: to stimulate the pride of the Dutch players before the return match. And it worked.

In an interview, Ruud Gullit explained: "I want to have people forgive me for this troubled season. Berlusconi will see that Van Basten and I are the best. And in any case, both of us scored a perfectly good goal in Madrid. Butragueno and Sanchez can't say the same."

On April 9, we drew 0-0 at the San Siro against a Napoli side who led us by four points. We wanted to reduce the gap to give us a shot at second place, but we didn't manage it. As I made clear in the log-book, we did not play well.

> *Flat performance without any kind of verve. When the team doesn't manage to shrug off markers and doesn't play at pace, there are obvious technical limitations: see our dribbling and one-twos. They also show limitations when it comes to character. No pressing. To improve: one-twos, dribbling, crossing, pressing, losing markers. We must help the forwards more.*

On April 15, four days before the second leg against Real, we also drew away to Lecce, with Virdis scoring our goal. That was an important game, because Filippo Galli returned after eight months out with injury. We gave him the last half hour or so. Having him back would allow me to restore Rijkaard to the midfield.

We approached the decisive match against Real Madrid with optimism, but in the very last training game the day before, fate played a horrible trick on us. The very young Demetrio Albertini went in hard on the ankle of Evani, who collapsed to the deck shouting and screaming and was carried off by his teammates. Demetrio was even more pale than Alberico, but he had nothing to be sorry for. I wanted every training match to be just like a proper game, with everyone bringing the same effort and the same grit. It would have been pointless otherwise. These kinds of accident could happen – it was something I had factored in.

The fact remained, however, that I'd lost our balancer for the most important game, one where we'd need to attack without exposing ourselves to the counter-attacking threat of Real's formidable forwards. I well-remembered how greatly we had missed Evani in the first leg against Red Star – I had even told the newspaper journalists as much. We didn't have another player in the squad with the same characteristics.

The most logical solution would have been to push Donadoni out to the flank – he'd often played wide – field Gullit as a No.10 and pair Virdis with Van Basten up front. I thought about it at length. For the first time ever, I asked the most senior players their opinion. But in the end I went with a solution which nobody had recommended: Ancelotti wide left.

Everyone knew he wasn't as quick off the mark as someone like Francisco Gento. Quite the opposite, in fact. When we did 50m sprint tests, he was often the slowest – up at around 8.5 seconds. Pinco and I would lie and tell him he'd done it in seven so that he didn't get too depressed.

One day we were working on overlaps. Gullit set off, and Ancelotti had to go beyond him to receive the pass. The first two times they tried it, the operation failed. Before the third, Carlo said to Ruud: "If you don't slow down a bit, I won't manage to go beyond you."

I knew fine well that Ancelotti didn't have the same

acceleration as Rijkaard or Gullit, who, athletically speaking, were two monsters. Once I had them do 200m shuttle runs together while Ramaccioni watched, dumbfounded. "Arrigo," he said. "If I had to choose between being hit by a scooter or by those two, I'd pick the scooter."

Whenever I put Ancelotti in the passing cage for a one-v-one match against Rijkaard, Carlo would always come out saying, "Boss, what did I do to upset you?"

I knew his battered legs weren't ideal for getting up and down the touchline, but you play football with your brain, not your feet. Ancelotti's brain would give us the right balance and timing. By staying tight and compact around him, the rest of the team would ensure he had minimal space to cover.

In the build-up to the match, I kept telling the players something I'd written in my log-book:

> *The best Milan did not manage to beat the worst Real Madrid. At the San Siro, the Spaniards can only play better.*

I didn't want my men to be lulled into a false sense of security by the good result from the first leg. Beenhakker kept saying that his team had the technical means to overcome our press, and he wasn't lying.

On the evening of April 19, 1989, San Siro was fuller and louder than I'd ever seen it – the perfect backdrop for such a big night. There were more than 73,000 people in the ground, and once again the world was looking in on TV. My team against the one I'd dreamed about as a kid.

Among those in the stands were two centrepieces of Milan history, Juan Alberto Schiaffino and Gianni Rivera. Gigi Riva was there too, and so was Paolo Pillitteri, the mayor of Milan, despite the fact he supported Inter. So, too, Enrico Ferri, the then minister for public works who famously imposed a 110km-per-hour speed limit on Italian motorways. Speaking to the press, he gave us a virtual ticket: "This Milan team exceeds all speed limits," he said.

Before the match, Berlusconi came down to the dressing room, where he was taken aback by a sudden roar. "It's coming from the Real Madrid lads," I explained. "Why don't we do the same?" he asked. "Those are cries of fear, Mr President."

CINEMA PARADISO

European Cup
Semi-final, second leg
Milan 5 Real Madrid 0

On the eve of the match, Berlusconi made a confession to the media. "I've asked my players to thrash them."

For him, it wasn't enough to beat Real Madrid and reach the European Cup final for the first time in 20 years. No – he expected us to thrash the most prestigious and successful club in the history of football. Berlusconi had true greatness in him. I'd understood this right from that first dinner at Arcore, and it was the shared love of big dreams and beauty which had immediately put us in synch.

Baresi was always wary of Berlusconi's pre-match press chats because he knew that the president could say anything. Every time, Franco would come and ask, "Boss, did the president speak today?"

"Yes," I would reply. "Well then, we better put on our helmets," Baresi would sigh, without even bothering to ask what Berlusconi had said.

On the eve of that Milan v Madrid showdown, when the president asked us to thrash them, that was his greatness in action. Juventus may have had directors who knew football better, but nobody knew life and beauty like Berlusconi, not least because at Juve, they've said for centuries that winning is the only thing that counts.

Our president understood football, but not enough to interfere in technical matters. In any case, he wouldn't have done that on a point of principle. It's simply not true that he tried to pick the team or sought to advocate for particular players. At least he never did with me. We disagreed about Borghi in the manner I've described, but at all other times he respected my work and never tried to influence it. And I can't recall a single occasion where he came into the dressing room to speak to a player. Indeed, the one and only time he came in before a match, he apologised afterwards.

We were playing KV Mechelen, the Belgians. Berlusconi appeared in the dressing room with two of his personal guests. The following day, he conceded: "I shouldn't have done that and I'm sorry. The dressing room is sacred."

That's 100% correct: it's one thing for the president to come in, quite another if it's outsiders.

Not long after he was appointed Fiorentina manager, Roberto Mancini came to the Italian federation's technical centre at Coverciano to ask me for some advice.

Firstly: "What should I do with Rui Costa? He's a No.10, but he's always coming back to pick up the ball."

I asked: "Is he willing to play in midfield?"

"No," Roberto replied.

"Well then, there's no solution."

Onto the second problem: "How should I keep in check the directors who try to interfere?"

"That's easy, Roberto," I replied. "Speak to them about

the game, not players. By doing that, you'll cut them out, because they don't have the knowledge to keep up."

The same was true of Berlusconi. I took care of the game, but he helped by pushing us towards beauty and dreams, training us to think big – asking us to thrash them when a 0-0 draw would have sufficed.

The evening of April 19, 1989 began with some real raw emotion. Four days previously, at Hillsborough Stadium in Sheffield, prior to the FA Cup semi-final between Liverpool and Nottingham Forest, 96 people had been crushed to death. The most painful tragedy in the history of British sport. During the minute's silence, the whole San Siro sang *You'll Never Walk Alone*. Many moving telegrams of thanks arrived from Liverpool in the subsequent days.

The game didn't start well for us, Real immediately creating a good chance. Beenhakker had played his joker card by fielding the extremely young Paco Llorente – Gento's nephew and just as quick off the mark. He was intended to be the arrow that evaded our press and surprised our defence with his pace.

We were struggling. Van Basten made a number of mistakes, prompting me to tell Virdis to warm up. The good Ramaccioni was worried and advised me: "Arrigo, hold on a little bit longer."

Slowly but surely, our game began to grow. With Ancelotti in Evani's position, a few of our reference points changed, but our principles remained the same. The ideas that guided everything we did were exactly the same, and in short order our pressing had Real Madrid by the throat, just as had been the case at the Bernabeu.

In the 18th minute, that man Carlo carried the ball from left to right, then set himself for a shot with a series of touches. Having closed in on goal, he let fly with a hard right-footed shot that sailed over Buyo's head and went in under the crossbar. A marvellous goal that inflamed the whole ground.

It was then Rijkaard's turn to score, with a powerful whip of his neck which sent a perfect Tassotti cross from the right into the back of the net. The third goal, right at the end of the first half, came from the left. Donadoni got away from his man by feigning to go back inside then sent over a delicate ball. Gullit pounced on it and, strong as an ox, crashed a header home, his dreadlocks being lifted up by the force.

Three-nil at the break: absolute dominance of play and beauty. The San Siro couldn't believe its collective eyes.

The fourth goal, a few minutes into the second half, was an all-Dutch production. Frank's cross, Ruud's knock-down, Marco's lovely control and unstoppable left-footed shot into the roof of the net.

At that point, Berlusconi was more than convinced that Gullit and Van Basten were the best, and that there was no reason to be envious of Hugo Sanchez and Butragueno. In actual fact, he'd known that before. The criticisms and comparisons the president had made after the match at the Bernabeu were intended to inject a bit of extra anger into the Dutch players' performances.

At 4-0 came the only bad news of the night. Ruud pulled up in midfield with a grimace of pain, holding his left knee. He sat down on the pitch and was carried off on a stretcher. Yet another injury in what, for him, was a truly cursed season.

Two days later, Professor Perugia operated on him in the Villa Bianca clinic in Rome. We were in the final, but with the fear that we would be missing two key cogs: Evani and

Gullit. In the hours immediately after the match at the San Siro, it was too early to worry about that. There was only room for joy and pride.

Donadoni came in off the right and hit a low left-footed show which Buyo, who was having a rather clumsy night, couldn't keep out. 5-0. Exactly the thrashing which Berlusconi had requested the day before! Indeed, in the post-match media session, the president went from interview to interview saying, "I told you so! I told you so!"

President Mendoza's prayer card had not been of any use. In a real touch of class, he embraced Berlusconi and promised him: "We'll be supporting you in Barcelona. You're a really strong team."

Berlusconi thanked him with tears in his eyes. I'd rarely seen him so moved and happy. The whole world had admired the beauty of his Milan.

Our fans stayed behind for a long time, singing and celebrating in the stands. It seemed like they were struggling to tear themselves away from the spectacular show they had just witnessed – they couldn't bring themselves to go home. Like actors who return to the stage after the final scene, Baresi and Rijkaard came back out of the dressing room and took to the pitch to thank the 80,000 people who were still applauding.

Milan v Real Madrid truly was one of – if not the – most exhilarating productions we put on. It was the one that gave us the most visibility across the world, and we showed a beauty that went well beyond the result. It was more like art.

A few days later, the director Giuseppe Tornatore won the Cannes Jury Prize for *Nuovo Cinema Paradiso (New Paradise Cinema,* released internationally as *Cinema Paradiso),* which had been in movie theatres the previous year. He would go on to win an Oscar in Los Angeles as well. With the same wide eyes as the young protagonist of the film, the San Siro crowd had borne witness to the *Nuovo Milan Paradiso*.

The next morning, my wife told me that I'd shouted "Goal!" five times in my sleep and woken her up on each occasion. Evidently, I'd watched the game back in my dreams. I'm absolutely sure I didn't add anything to the beauty of what actually happened – that would have been impossible.

My log-book shows just how satisfied I was. Three times in one entry I used the word "excellent".

> *Excellent match, excellent result, team in excellent physical and mental shape.*

I still found something to improve…

> *Positional interchange in midfield, between the right and left central midfielders. We need more rotations to avoid giving reference points to the markers. And we also need more movement without the ball.*

On the Thursday night, I went for dinner with president Berlusconi at Assassino, a favoured *Milanisti* haunt in the middle of town where Nereo Rocco often used to eat. That evening, at our table was also Arnaldo Forlani, the former Christian Democracy prime minister.

As far as luck is concerned, I take Seneca's line that it does not exist. If anything, we're talking about a moment when talent meets opportunity. I believe I've taken my opportunities well. If I hadn't played Milan so many times as manager of Parma, I probably would not have become Berlusconi's coach. If my Milan team hadn't played Real

Madrid four times in the space of a few months, we probably would not have achieved the global visibility which we earned through those matches.

I once said to my friend Butragueno: "Emilio, your Real team seemed to me like Lorenzo Zagonari who lost 18 snooker matches in a row. We always played each other and you guys never won. I felt like saying: 'let's play one more because I'm really not convinced my Milan are the better team.'"

IF WE PLAY WELL, WE WIN

The following Sunday, we had the derby. Gullit, who had undergone midweek surgery in Rome and been visited by Ancelotti – a connoisseur of operating theatres – sent us a message. "There can't be 12 points between us and Inter."

At the end of the match, Nicola Berti hit back in his own way. "We're not Real Madrid."

A derby that was more a battle than a game finished 0-0. Among the few exciting moments was the 'usual' ghost goal that was not awarded. This time it was Ancelotti, who hit a real fireball to match the one he'd scored with against Real. The speed cameras measured it at 103 kmph. It struck the underside of the bar, bounced down over the line then bounced back out.

We got a fright with Rijkaard, who fell awkwardly, hit his head off the ground and was taken to hospital, where he spent the night.

I had expected a drop in motivation after the exhilarating tussle with Real, which delivered us to the biggest of days in Barcelona. I said as much in the post-match interviews and in my diary too.

> *Good first 10 minutes, acceptable next 10, then the team began to play ever more slowly with few runs off the ball. They didn't often look to win the ball or for space, preferring to wait for the ball in a static position. Our distributors slowed everything down and those receiving the ball didn't move at the right times. As such, we were easy to stop and susceptible to counter-attacks. Our pressing was non-existent. The one good thing: among the crowd was Anghel Iordanescu, the Steaua Bucharest coach. We played like he's hoping we will in Barcelona.*

But I already knew that we would grow as the final drew nearer, and that on the day of the game, we would not let ourselves down. As always. And indeed, in the following games, we slowly got better.

May 7: Milan 2-1 Torino, with goals from Colombo and Van Basten, who showed off his Ballon d'Or trophy to the San Siro crowd.

> *Slow and indolent first half. Better second half, especially with regards to possession – fast, probing moves. Pressing needs to improve and we need more three-man central attacks to avoid the usual cross.*

Maldini sprained his ankle and would be out for eight days. That was our biggest worry: losing more players with less and less time to get them back. We were already battling against the clock to have Evani and Gullit on the field in Barcelona. Ruud had flown back to Holland to see his physiotherapist friend Troost.

At the end of the game, Berlusconi – who always had something to say about other teams' strikers – eulogised the Brazilian, Muller. "He moves like a cat. If only I could buy him."

Perhaps he wanted to repeat the strategy which had paid off against Real Madrid: make Gullit and Van Basten jealous so that they responded with goals.

May 14: Sampdoria 1-1 Milan, a goal from Rijkaard. I wrote in my log-book:

> *Team in good physical condition, but with their heads already in Barcelona. Inattentive and lacking intensity as a result. Lots of errors in marking and very little pressing. Good result, poor performance.*

The truth was that everyone – including the fans – already had their heads in Barcelona. Some 15,000 tickets were put on sale for the final and they disappeared in the space of two hours. Lots of supporters slept on the pavement to secure their place in the queue.

On May 20 at the San Siro, four days before the European Cup final, we had our dress rehearsal. I had back both Evani, who played the full 90 minutes, and Gullit, who got the last half hour. Chicco was still a long way from his best form, while Ruud explained to the media: "I'm at 60%. I'll play in Barcelona, but I don't know for how long or how well." We drew 0-0 with Cesena.

A read of the log-book would also make you think we'd had a very negative, alarming dress rehearsal.

Ugly game. Demotivated and inattentive team. Van Basten needs to make more diagonal runs at the right time. Not go long twice then short 50 times.

When I got back home, my wife said: "Phone the president straight away. He's called you at least six times."

Berlusconi was really worried: "Arrigo, did you see how we played?"

I sought to calm him down, saying: "Mr President, the trouble is that the human brain can only focus intensely on one thing at a time. And our heads are already in Barcelona. But we're absolutely fine, trust me. We never mess up the important games."

I gave the players a rest the following day. On the morning of Monday, May 22, we turned our attention to Steaua Bucharest.

Everyone had us as favourites, but we couldn't afford to underestimate a team who only three years previously had won the European Cup, beating Barcelona in another final played in Spain (Seville). Steaua had scored five goals over the two legs of their semi-final against Galatasaray, reaching the showpiece in imperious fashion. They were a good team who knew how to dribble and had some excellent individual players like Marius Lacatus – quick – and the really technical Gheorghe Hagi.

Across a couple of pages of my log-book, I made a series of random observations about the Romanians which I used to inform our work and the players' instructions. Here are some of them:

Use a lot of one-twos on the edge of the box as well as 'one comes short, the other goes long'. They use a static system where everyone goes deep. Their defensive line is not very dynamic and they struggle to deal with pressing. When attacked, they're badly positioned. We need to stay compact and not let them hit us on the break. They try to make you come out by making you angry and annoyed. They often pass back the way, and struggle to cope with pace and counter-attacks. You can attack them by going deep, but they are dangerous on the break through the speed of Hagi and Lacatus. Good in tight areas and at keeping the ball. They take corners with two men. Numbers four and six are strong at high balls. At corners, six of them will be in the box to jump. Hagi takes centre-right free-kicks and right-sided corners and puts spin on the ball. On the left, they'll touch free-kicks to Stefan Iovan. Lacatus has an excellent long throw and is good at attacking in behind. Their two central defenders are slow. We need to stay compact and attack them – that way, they won't be able to get out. They struggle to cope with pace and tempo.

Inspired by these observations, on Monday, May 22 at Milanello we worked hard on – for example – the movement of our two forwards: "One comes short, the other goes long."

Stefan Iovan and Adrian Bumbescu were slow centre-backs who struggled to get out and intercept opponents. The defensive line, in turn, struggled to cover their movements.

In the following year's final, against Benfica in Vienna, we encountered a similar pair of central defenders, Aldair and Ricardo Gomes, and that very movement led to our winning goal: Costacurta came out with the ball and Van Basten dropped back to meet him. Rijkaard slipped into the space he left behind and scored the game's only goal.

That Monday I inked another couple of thoughts into my log-book. The first was my recipe for an antidote to the mounting tension as we approached the final:

> *We need to be numb to any emotion, focusing only on the things we need to do and doing them to the best of our abilities.*

That meant using our whole brains to study and revise our knowledge, not leaving any space for anything else. We needed to stop our minds turning to thoughts of worry or any other negative sentiment.

If you are completely focused on the movements you need to show in the game, and if you convince yourself you have memorised in training the right reaction to any situation which the game can throw up, you'll feel ready and safe from fear.

My second thought may seem totally obvious, even infantile, but it is the key to everything. The heart of our mission and our philosophy.

> *Play well. If we play well, we win. If they play better, they'll win.*

We didn't just want to win. It wasn't enough to bring home the European Cup after an absence of 20 years. We wanted to deserve our victory, using the strength of our values. We wanted to succeed through our strategy, not with sly tactics. We were ready to hail the merits of our opponents if they played better than us.

> *Play well. If we play well, we win.*

The training session on Tuesday, May 23 consisted of:

> 10v10 handball training match on a 40x25m pitch (goals can only be scored with the head)
> Five minutes of crossing and shooting
> More work on 'one comes short, one goes long'
> 15 minutes of 11v11 game on a small pitch to train our reactiveness and play in tight areas.

That afternoon, we boarded an Alitalia jumbo jet at Malpensa and set off for Barcelona. My wife, Giovanna, and daughter, Federica, were with me, and also on board were a pregnant Luisa Ancelotti, and the wives of Gullit, Giovanni Galli and other players. I remember little Niccolò Galli* running around everywhere. He was six at the time and would have become a good player had a terrible fate not taken him away from us at such a young age.

Cesare Maldini – who had just become a grandfather – was there too, as was Enzo Bearzot, and the former Italian federation president Federico Sordillo. Also present were Gianni Rivera, Renzo Burini, Giancarlo 'Panther' Danova, Ettore Puricelli and Albino Buticchi. Not to mention the Duke of Aosta with his wife, a Sicilian countess. There were also lots of journalists. Franco Baresi read, and so did Virdis, while the Dutch players played their usual game of backgammon.

On the morning of the final, Wednesday May 24, there were 20,000 fans packed into the little stadium beside Camp Nou for our final training session. Incredible

---

* Niccolò, son of Giovanni, died aged 17 in February 2001 in a road accident while driving back from a session at Bologna's training centre. He was a promising defender who had won the FA Youth Cup with Arsenal the previous year

enthusiasm. Nobody had ever seen a training session with that kind of backdrop before.

10 minutes of stretching
10 minutes on attack
Game of one-touch piggy in the middle
5v2 on a 10x10m pitch – fast and intense
Five minutes on shooting

Gullit came to tell me: “Boss, Iordanescu, the Steaua coach, is here watching.”

I replied: “It doesn’t matter, because when it comes to the match, you guys never reproduce what we try in training.”

However, when we came to practise penalties at the end, I told them: “Take one properly, then muck up the second.”

Practising penalties is worthwhile up to a point, but it’s not just a matter of technique. In a game, other factors come into play when you step up to the spot. One of them is emotion, sure, but even more important is the sense of justice which comes over you.

In the 1994 World Cup final, Brazil deserved more than us. We gave everything we had, the very last drop of energy – there was nothing more we could have given. But they played better and quite rightly won on penalties. When they stepped up to take their kicks, they felt like they were on the right side of history. We did not.

Barcelona was swamped by a 90,000-strong red and black tide. That night, we crossed it in our bus while mounted police made way using their truncheons. Berlusconi prayed in the Camp Nou chapel, denouncing the Steaua communists to the eternal father.

The German referee, Karl-Heinz Tritschler, blew his whistle and the European Cup final was under way.

THE FINAL – ACT TWO

European Cup final
Steaua Bucharest 0 Milan 4
Barcelona, May 24, 1989

Straight away, Donadoni scared their goalkeeper, Silviu Lung, with a shot from the edge of the box. Van Basten came mighty close with a header and Gullit struck a post.

We grabbed Steaua Bucharest by the throat from the very first minute and never let go. We just didn't stop. We were always moving forward, whether or not we had the ball. That was our strategy: we had a positive plan that we wanted to carry out. We wanted to impose our ideas, our values, and earn this great trophy.

By contrast, the Romanians looked to hurt us using tactics. They thought they'd identified our weak spot, and moved Hagi – their strongest player – into Ancelotti's zone, believing they could cause him difficulty on the flank.

But Carlo was never alone. He always had two or three teammates around him to cut down the space he had to cover, and then he had the intelligence and the timing to do his job in the best possible fashion. As had been the case with Maradona, Hagi ended up thinking of Ancelotti as a quick bloke with a No.11 on his back.

In the 18th minute, Colombo has a shot from the right of the box which the goalkeeper can't hold. Van Basten pounces on the ball, and the rebound lands at the feet of Gullit, who tucks in the opening goal. The roar of the crowd makes the Barcelona sky shake.

A year previously, when they were calling me Mr Nobody, who could possibly have imagined that we would score in the European Cup final thanks to a shot from Angelo Colombo?

Less than 10 minutes later, Tassotti makes ground on the right flank, working the ball with the sole of his foot like a Brazilian winger. He dribbles, goes to the line and delivers a silky cross. I want to make clear that I did not do much work on those feet. I found them already well educated by the great technical efforts of Nils Liedholm. When Tassotti stands the ball up, Gullit attacks the front post while Van Basten moves towards the far, depositing a thumping header into the net.

In the 39th minute, three or four white shirts surround the Romanian with the ball and take it off his toes. Pressing: our true soul. Donadoni looks up and picks out Gullit at the edge of the box with a precise left-footed ball. Ruud controls it, lets it bounce then crashes home.

Camp Nou, covered in red and black banners, is totally delirious. Everything seems easy, beautiful, perfect: we're 3-0 up at the break.

In the dressing room, I order: "Let's get a fourth, then we can slow down and manage the game from there."

The fourth arrives almost immediately, a minute after the restart. Rijkaard – the guy preferred to Borghi – moves forward and plays in Van Basten, who lets the ball run before hitting it on the diagonal into the far corner. The game is done and dusted.

Not long before full-time, Berlusconi leaves his seat in the stand and comes pitchside. Waiting for the final whistle, he kneels next to the silk-covered table on which the European Cup is sitting. It's almost like he is standing guard over a trophy he now considers his.

Tritschler blows for full-time and the party can well and truly begin. The president runs towards me, embraces me and the first thing he says is: "I've never spent my money in a better way!"

He's talking about the salary increase he now owes me: three times the difference between what they gave me and what I had asked for. Those were the terms of our bet and I'd won.

I enter the field then hug Galliani and each of my players in turn. I take Van Basten by the legs and lift him off the ground. I do the same to Gullit. Me, the little guy, raising my two giants to the sky.

It's got nothing to do with the adrenaline or enthusiasm of our triumph. There's nothing magic or absurd about that strength. The secret was the same as always: hard work. In those days, I could bench press 105kg. The two Dutch players each weighed less than 90kg. The sums make sense.

Speaking to the media, Berlusconi recites a line of Horace in Latin: "Tomorrow once again we sail the ocean sea."

People derided him when he promised to conquer the world while showing it a good time. In the meantime, he had already conquered Europe. Without his ability to think big, to hunt down dreams, we would not have been there celebrating in the middle of Camp Nou. Right from that first dinner at Arcore, the president and I shared the same idea of greatness and we managed to bring the team with us, transforming our ambitious horizons into a shared challenge.

Milan have won the club's third European Cup, we're bringing the trophy back for the first time in 20 years. I'd be lying if I said it's a dream come true, because all this goes well beyond a dream. From childhood, I've been able to dream about a triumph, but not this kind, not this way. I didn't have the capacity to imagine all this.

In our last three games, the two legs of the semi-final and the final itself, we've scored 10 goals and conceded one, from a corner. Against Steaua, we had 21 shots on goal. We've graced the stage with beauty, we've played better than our opponents and we've won with merit, bringing our values to bear.

It's time for the trophy presentation. The team gathers round captain Franco Baresi, who grabs the cup by the ears and lifts it into the sky. He's got a No.6 on his back.

My coaching career began with that number, at Fusignano, 16 years previously. I told Alfredo I needed a sweeper. The Corellian librarian found a No.6 jersey in the dressing room, gave it to me and said: "Build one for yourself, with ideas and hard work."

And now the best sweeper in the world, wearing a No.6 shirt, is lifting up a European Cup won by those self-same ideas and hard work. In front of Alfredo Belletti, who came to Barcelona with that Co-op plastic bag.

Berlusconi leaves the stadium on the team bus. He thinks it's going to be a triumphal march, like the one on the way here, and he doesn't want to miss out this time. But everyone is already celebrating back in town and there's no need for truncheons to clear our path.

I hug my wife and daughter. We go to toast the success

with some friends who have come from Italy. When I get back to the hotel, I pick up my log-book and for the first time since I started compiling it, I write a single word. Just one.

Fantastic!

A TASTE OF HONEY

We came back to Italy the following day. My wife stayed in Milan, while I went to Fusignano. On the motorway, I passed dozens of buses carrying red-and-black-clad supporters home from their glorious trip to Barcelona. Our 90,000-strong army.

I was driving really fast: 160-170kmph. Near Bologna, I realised that a police car was following me with blue flashing lights.

"Oh no, here we go…"

I pulled over, resigned to being ticketed. However, the driver of the vehicle was the deputy commander of the Bologna police, a keen Milan fan who had recognised and pursued me purely to offer his congratulations.

That night I went to bed and the following morning, after a deep and peaceful sleep, I awoke to absolute silence: my wife wasn't in and my daughters had gone to school.

A really strange thing happened that I would never again experience in my whole life – I woke up with the sweet taste of honey in my mouth. Inexplicable but absolutely unmistakeable.

On May 27, Berlusconi invited me to Rimini for a meeting of one of his financial companies. He'd ordered in two other new European champions: Gullit and Donadoni. He kept us hidden to begin with, so that he could create one of those moments of great surprise of which he is so fond.

"I think I recognise that big bloke with the dreadlocks," he announced at a certain point from the stage. Gullit came forth from the back of the room amid a deluge of applause. Next it was Donadoni's turn, then mine.

"We'll be top of the world before long, right Arrigo?" Berlusconi said.

"Absolutely," I replied.

It was nice to come back to Rimini as a European champion. It was in that city that I'd experienced one of my most important – and certainly most difficult – seasons. My first in Serie C, coming straight from coaching the Cesena Reserves.

When my name started to appear as a possible candidate for the role of manager, a local journalist welcomed me by listing a load of other names (Antonio Angelillo, Lauro Toneatto, Angelo Domenghini, Domenico Rosati). Right at the end he added mine, before opening a parenthesis: "But let's not mention certain names…"

The Rimini directors had followed the two legs of the Reserve League final and had been enchanted by my Cesena team, who played really well. After beating Inter in the semi-finals, we faced Avellino for the national title. The Rimini directors watched those games because they had sold defender Luciano Favero – a future European Cup winner – to Avellino and as part of the deal they had the right to choose two players from the Avellino reserves. This was their chance to take a look at potential candidates.

They would end up choosing well: Nando De Napoli and Marco Pecoraro Scanio, brother of Alfonso, the former leader of the Italian Green Party. Marco would himself later become a senator with the same party.

I reached an agreement with the Rimini directors and took the reins of their first team. Our debut match was in the Coppa Italia against Inter, who only won in added time thanks to a Hansi Muller free-kick. That was August 1982, and the joy from Italy's World Cup win was still in the air.

My first three league games were draws, firstly at home to Mestre, then with the Carrarese team coached by Corrado Orrico and finally against Modena. Our fourth match saw us win away to Brescia, the big favourites for the title. Back home the following week, the Rimini crowd – largely made up of out-of-season lifeguards – welcomed us with great applause. They assumed we would be relegated, but we finished fourth – a good season.

Against Carrarese, I'd surprised the fans by fielding five or six young players, who were more receptive to my new ideas. Guys like Gianluca Gaudenzi, Nando De Napoli, Davide Zannoni, with all the old blokes moving to the bench.

At the end of the match, I was asked: "Boss, why did you stay standing for the whole game today?"

"Because the bench was red hot," I replied.

In Rimini, a manager has the added responsibility of keeping an eye on his players away from the pitch, because the city is an amusement park. I lived close to the sea and to get home I had to pass the sign placed at the entrance to the area with all the bars and clubs, which read: "We inform you that you are now entering the fakes zone."

The fake and the show-off are two hedonists who like to boast about their feats. The difference is that the show-off can do what he says he can, while the fake is precisely that – a fake.

Pecoraro Scanio, thinking I was some kind of fucking idiot, would always introduce a different woman to me as his girlfriend.

Once I said to one of those girls: "The last time I saw you, you were blonde."

She replied: "But I've never been blonde."

From that day forth, Pecoraro stopped introducing me to his girlfriends.

On my journey home, I would be driving towards the sea, so I'd train my headlights on the beach then turn around and head off. One night, in the beam I saw Daniele Zoratto leaning against one of the beach club huts. Between Zoratto and the cabin there was a woman, taller than him. I was instantly able to explain the calf pains that afflicted him – he was always on his tip-toes.

Zoratto, in truth, had a heart of gold and was an excellent midfielder. The first time I saw him play in the sixth-tier Promozione league, I thought: "There are guys in Serie A who can't do what you do."

He then went to Serie C, where he didn't do well, because they paid him 50,000 lire a month (approx 25 Euros) and he could only eat one meal per day. He came from a poor family – his father was a miner in Luxembourg and for a long time Daniele had lived with his grandmother in Italy. When I brought him to Cesena, he asked: "Would you mind sorting out my salary with the president? I'm ashamed to ask for money to play football." He thought about his father down the mine and felt ashamed.

I brought him to Rimini and gave him his national team cap as well. I explained to the Rimini president: "I understand your budget problems. If you need to rebuild the squad from scratch each year, I won't complain. I only ask one thing: that you don't sell Zoratto. You can sell anyone else, but not him. I'll build the new team around him."

One game out from the end of the first league season, the Rimini president invited me for lunch at a restaurant called The Madman, run by a bloke who truly was insane. In the middle of August, he would put his car in the middle of the courtyard under the baking sun, then climb in for a sauna. But his food was good.

The president explained that he had been forced to sell Zoratto. That same night, I phoned Italo Allodi and told him that I would come to coach the youth section of his Fiorentina.

It was nice, though, to be back in Rimini as a newly-minted European champion, reliving so many memories from the start of my career journey.

The official party for our European Cup win took place at the end of the season at Silvio Berlusconi's Arcore villa. My wife was very emotional when she entered that place, because she knew that Villa San Martino had been built by the Casati Stampa family and belonged to Marquess Camillo who, in 1970, killed his wife and her young lover before taking his own life. It was a truly landmark crime which had long filled the newspapers and magazines when Giovanna was a girl.

Berlusconi gave each of the women a jewel, which he fished from a silver tray. These weren't just any old jewels, but ones he had chosen himself for each of the invited ladies. For Giovanna, he'd selected a brooch which resembled the European Cup. It was a vase, made up of coloured gemstones, which resembled the shape of the trophy.

Lots of the women must have been accustomed to that kind of gift and gave thanks in a very calm fashion. For Giovanna, it was a real novelty which made a big impression on her, augmenting the emotion caused by the invisible presence of the tormented Marquess Casati Stampa which roamed from room to room.

Berlusconi's gift to me was a life-size silver replica of the European Cup, engraved with his signature. On my way home after midnight, I headed for Corso Buenos Aires to buy the newspapers hot off the press. When I spied a kiosk on the other side of the road, I made a U-turn and this lad, who was travelling at some speed and couldn't stop, hit my car full on.

Nobody was hurt – Giovanna went home in a taxi while I took care of the formalities. The kid was freaked out, however. He'd taken his brother's car without telling him to go out with his girlfriend, and he didn't know how to break the news. He kept apologising, not least because he was a Milan fan and felt bad about causing me problems after everything we'd done in Barcelona. I tried to calm him down, saying that I'd been the careless one and that everything would work out fine. Several passers-by came over, offering to help fit the Porsche's spare tyre after one of the original ones was punctured in the collision. As we worked, on the other side of the road a car flashed by with its windows down. The driver, probably an Inter fan, shouted: "Arrigo, the fog won't save you this time!"

I keep my 1989 European Cup replica, the one from 1990 and all the other trophies that I won as a manager or director, in my home gym. They are all together on a raised shelf above the door. The only thing that's missing is the Coppa Italia I won as a Parma director.

I once asked my Milan players: "When we started out, did you expect to win so much and to receive so much recognition? They voted us the best team in history."

Everyone said no apart from Tasso who, with his incomparable sense of irony, remarked: "With all the work you made us do, it was the least we deserved."

Recently, *France Football* magazine chose the 50 most important managers of all-time and put me in third place, behind Rinus Michels and Alex Ferguson but ahead of Johan Cruyff and Pep Guardiola. Two of my players also made the list: Ancelotti in eighth place and Rijkaard in 45th. Explaining my ranking, *France Football* stated: "His tactical approach changed the mentality of a whole country."

A few days later, Berlusconi rang to wish me a happy birthday, and I told him my news. "Are you proud, Mr President? Your manager is No.3 in the all-time history books." He told me I should go into politics. "All the Milan fans would vote for you."

My reply? "Mr President, I don't have your stamina. I need a quiet life."

The son of Jesus Gil, the Atletico Madrid president, once came to see me in Fusignano and asked: "How many years did it take you to win all this? Atletico has a hundred years of history but we don't have as many trophies."

I look at those trophies while I pedal on my exercise bike. I'm stationary, but it's like I'm moving towards them. I look at them and feel less tired. I'm not proud of those pieces of metal, but of the ideas, the values and the hard work they represent. And the men who lived those values: The Immortals.

Those trophies are the proof that, as I wrote in the pages of my log-book, the team that plays better wins. I watch them as I run or pedal in my gym, and every so often there is a slight taste of honey in my mouth.

BACKPAGE

"Pirlo's autobiography is like an erotic novel for football fans"

Four Four Two

"The autobiography of Andrea Pirlo displays a mischievous wit and an acute gift for observation"

Richard Williams, The Guardian

"Footballing autobiographies are not generally at the forefront of literary output, but this one is a superb read"

Jim White, The Telegraph

PEP'S CITY
THE MAKING OF A SUPERTEAM
'Stunning insight . . . brilliant access and superbly told stories'
DANIEL TAYLOR
POL BALLÚS
& LU MARTÍN